Hands-On English

Written by Fran Santoro Hamilton

Illustrated by Michael Hamilton

PORTICO
BOOKS

Portico Books, P. O. Box 9451, St. Louis, MO 63117

Copy Editing by Marnie Hauff

Cover Design by Mandy Roberts, Helleny Graphic Design, Earth City, MO

Printing and Binding by Comfort-Fiedler Printing, St. Louis, MO

First printing 1998

10 9 8 7 6 5 4 3 2

Printed in the United States of America

Library of Congress Cataloging-in-Publication Data
Hamilton, Fran Santoro
   Hands-On English / Fran Santoro Hamilton
      p.   cm.
   Includes index
   ISBN: 0-9664867-0-6
   1. English language—Grammar—Handbooks, manuals, etc.
   I. Title.
PE1097.H35 1998

428.24—dc20   CIP 98-091479

Dedicated

to all who grapple with the English language—

in work or in play

ACKNOWLEDGMENTS

Many people contributed to *Hands-On English* to such a large extent that the book probably would not have come into being without them. First of all, I thank the students I have taught over the past twenty years. They shaped the book's content by showing me the information they needed. I am also grateful to their parents and to my colleagues, who frequently acclaimed the forerunner of *Hands-On English*, which I used in my classroom for nine years. I thank Pat Broderick and Leslie Kerr for their suggestions for revising that prototype (suggestions that were underappreciated at the time they were given because they necessitated much work). I thank Yvonne Suess for help with the design of *Hands-On English* and for being readily available to answer questions related to graphics. I thank Alicia Nolte, Doug Nolte, Trudie Olsen, and Bill Olsen for giving feedback on various features of the book along the way and for helping me venture into technical realms that were foreign to me. I thank the St. Louis Publishers Association and Dan Malan for teaching me about the process of publishing, and I thank Dan Poynter for *The Self-Publishing Manual*, a guide which has proven worthy of all the trust I placed in it. I thank my son Mike for the creativity and patience that enabled him to graphically depict parts of speech and to generate the other illustrations that help to reinforce the concepts in *Hands-On English*. Finally, I thank both of my sons— Mike and John—for their unflagging confidence and encouragement. With their example—as well as their words—they have continually said, "Go for it!"

TABLE OF CONTENTS

TO THE USER OF THIS BOOK

Congratulations! You are lucky to be one of over 700,000,000 users of the English language.* About half of those people learn English as their first language. However, more people speak English as their *second* language than any other language on earth.

English is spoken around the globe. It is used by pilots and air traffic controllers at international airports. Most printed and electronic communication, and most scientific and technical publications are written in English.

How did English come to be such an international language? Just as the United States is made up of people who have come from many nations, English includes words that have come from many languages. For centuries traders and warriors have carried their languages wherever they went. English was heavily influenced by Greek, Latin, French, and German. However, the roots of English go all the way back to ancient India!

When England began establishing colonies around the globe in the sixteenth century, her sailors and settlers took the English language with them. Some people they encountered learned English, and English, in turn, adopted many words from other languages.

See if you can match each English word in the list on the left below with its language of origin in the list on the right. (You can check your answers in a dictionary.)

aardvark	Afrikaans
alphabet	Arabic
bungalow	Bengali
camel	Cantonese
canyon	French
kindergarten	German
permission	Greek
shampoo	Hawaiian
ski	Hebrew
souvenir	Hindi
typhoon	Latin
ukulele	Norwegian
zero	Spanish

---

*Much of this information about English appeared in Richard Lederer's book *The Miracle of Language* (New York: Pocket Books, 1991), pages 19-32.

The preceding list contains only a small sample of the tens of thousands of colorful words that the English language has adopted from its colleagues.

Because English adopts words so freely, English has many more words than other languages have. Comprehensive English dictionaries list approximately half a million words. If technical, scientific, slang, and specialized words were added, the number would be about two million! Other major languages have fewer than 200,000 words; French, fewer than 100,000.

Because we have so many words from so many places, we often have many choices about how to say something. (A thesaurus will bring these choices to your fingertips.) Blue, for example, could be navy, turquoise, aquamarine, ultramarine, azure, cobalt, steel, or indigo.

The disadvantage of having words from so many languages is that English has many spellings that seem to be irregular. Consider, for example, how many different ways a particular sound, such as ō, can be spelled—or how many ways a particular spelling, such as *ough* can be pronounced.

I hope *Hands-On English* will provide you with quick access to the information you need (or want) about English. The table of contents will show you how the book is organized, and the index will help you find information on particular topics. Some sections of the book, such as the list of irregular verbs or the meanings of morphemes, would be good for you to study on your own.

I love to get letters, and I would love to hear from *you*. Please let me know what you liked about this book and how it helped you. I would also like to know if you have suggestions for improving the book. Is there information you were looking for that you did not find? Is there information that was unclear? Did you find an error?

I hope *Hands-On English* will help you to become a linguiphile or a verbivore. Those are terms that you probably will not find in a dictionary. If you find out what they mean, there's a good chance you have already become one!

Fran Hamilton
Portico Books
P.O. Box 9451
St. Louis, MO 63117

GRAMMAR

Without being aware of it, you have been using grammar since you were a baby. When you first began to make sense of the things your parents were saying to you, you began to understand grammar. After hearing words like *boys*, *girls*, *dogs*, and *cats*, you learned that an *s* at the end of some words makes them mean "more than one." You then applied this rule to form many other plurals. You probably even applied this rule to some words that form their plurals in other ways. You might have said *foots* instead of *feet*, for example, or *mouses* instead of *mice*. As you heard and read the English language over the years, you learned more about its rules and patterns.

Words are the building blocks of language. Although individual words have their own meanings, most communication uses words in combination. Word order is a very important part of grammar. How many different ideas can you communicate by combining the following words in different ways?

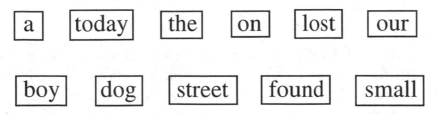

Using all of the words in each sentence, you should be able to make at least eight different sentences.

1

Becoming more familiar with the structure of language—with grammar—will make language easier for you to use—whether you are listening, talking, reading, writing, or just thinking.

PARTS OF SPEECH

Words can be classified into eight groups called **parts of speech.** Each part of speech has a specific job to do. A word's part of speech depends on the word's job in a particular sentence. A word, such as *run*, may be one part of speech in one sentence and a different part of speech when it is working differently in another sentence.

NOUNS

A **noun** is a word which names a person, a place, a thing, or an idea.

Persons: girl, uncle, cashier, chairperson, friend

Places: park, school, city, fairgrounds, kitchen

Things: building, stereo, puppy, week, hamburger

Ideas: love, democracy, loyalty, truth, sadness

A word ending in *-ness*, *-ment*, *-tion*, *-sion*, or *-ion* is usually a noun.

happi**ness**   apart**ment**   atten**tion**   divi**sion**   un**ion**

In this book we use a block to represent a noun. Nouns may be classified as **common nouns** or **proper nouns.** The nouns listed above are common nouns. They name persons, places, things, or ideas in general. A proper noun names a particular person, place, thing, or idea and begins with a capital letter. Examples of proper nouns are listed at the top of the next page.

Persons: Uncle Joe, Mrs. Simmons, President Adams

Places: Forest Park, Lincoln School, Clayton Road

Things: Sears Tower, Lassie, Porsche, Big Mac

Ideas: Christianity, Judaism, Islam, Hinduism

PRONOUNS

A **pronoun** is a word that is <u>used in place of a noun</u>. Because a pronoun is so similar to a noun, in this book we use a shaded block to represent a pronoun. Pronouns help you to avoid repeating words. No pronouns are used in the following paragraph.

> *Felipe and John worked on a social studies project together. Felipe and John worked at Felipe's house one day after school. Felipe's mom offered Felipe and John some cookies before Felipe and John began work.*

The paragraph sounds much smoother when pronouns are used.

> *Felipe and John worked on a social studies project together. **They** worked at Felipe's house one day after school. **His** mom offered **them** some cookies before **they** began work.*

The noun a pronoun stands for must always be clear. In the paragraph above, *his* stands for *Felipe's*, and *they* and *them* stand for *Felipe and John*. <u>The noun a pronoun stands for</u> (called an **antecedent**) <u>does not need to be in the same sentence with the pronoun.</u> Antecedents are not clear in the following sentences.

> ***They** said **it** couldn't be done.* (Who said what couldn't be done? No nouns are used.)

> *Kate loaned **her** ruler to Liz. **She** said **it** didn't have*

3

metric markings. (Who said the ruler didn't have metric markings? Whether *she* refers to *Kate* or *Liz* is unclear.)

The chart on page 5 shows the most common pronouns, called **personal pronouns**. There are several other kinds of pronouns as well.

Indefinite pronouns, listed below, are less specific than personal pronouns. Often they do not refer to a particular noun.

all	both	each	someone
some	few	either	everyone
none	several	neither	anybody
	many	one	

Demonstrative pronouns demonstrate, or point out. The use of these words as adjectives is discussed on pages 58 and 59.

this	that	these	those

Interrogative pronouns are used to ask questions.

who	whom	what	which	whose

Reflexive pronouns are formed by adding *self* or *selves* to some personal pronouns.

myself	yourself	himself	herself	itself
ourselves	yourselves	themselves		

Notice that *hisself* and *theirselves* are not acceptable in standard usage. A reflexive pronoun may be used to carry action back to its antecedent or to emphasize its antecedent.

Allison rewarded herself with a ten-minute break.

Jim wanted to do the job himself.

I myself have never been outside the United States.

PERSONAL PRONOUNS

	S I N G U L A R			P L U R A L		
	Subjective	Objective	Possessive	Subjective	Objective	Possessive
1st person	I	me	my, mine	we	us	our, ours
2nd person	you	you	your, yours	you	you	your, yours
3rd person	he she it	him her it	his her, hers its	they	them	their, theirs

First person refers to the speaker (or writer): *I am happy. We are happy.*
Second person refers to the person spoken *to*: *You are my best friend. You are all invited to the party.*
Third person refers to a person or thing spoken *about*: *She is going to the party. They are going to the party.*
  (*She* and *they* are neither the persons speaking nor the persons spoken to.)

Only **subjective pronouns** should be used as the subject of a sentence or after a linking verb.
Only **objective pronouns** should be used as a direct object, an indirect object, or the object of a preposition.
Possessive pronouns are used to show ownership. In a sentence they work like adjectives, telling "which one."
  Notice that no possessive pronoun contains an apostrophe, not even *its*.

ADJECTIVES

An **adjective** <u>modifies, or describes, a noun or pronoun</u>. It answers one of these questions: <u>What kind? Which one? How many?</u>

   Three large red *trucks rolled down **that steep** hill.*

Large and *red* describe *trucks*. They tell "what kind" of trucks. *Three* also describes *trucks*. It tells "how many." *Steep* tells "what kind" of hill. *That* tells "which" hill. An adjective can change the picture created by a noun. Therefore, in this book we use paint (which can change the appearance of a block) to represent an adjective.

To find which word an adjective describes, ask yourself which noun or pronoun it is telling more about. You can also make a question using the adjective and the word *what*: TWO WHAT? LARGE WHAT? The answer to your question tells which word is being described, in this case *trucks*.

Sometimes an adjective comes after a word it describes instead of before it. If the adjective follows a linking verb (explained on pages 7 and 8), it is called a **predicate adjective**. Predicate adjectives are further discussed on pages 26 and 27.

   *The stamp is **old**.* (*Old* tells "what kind" of stamp.)

   *The photo, **old** and **tattered**, was **precious**.* (*Old, tattered,* and *precious* all describe *photo. Precious* is a predicate adjective.)

The most frequently used adjectives are *a, an,* and *the.* They are called **articles** or **noun markers**, and they tell "which one" or "how many."

A **verb** is a word that expresses <u>action</u> or a "<u>state of being</u>." **Action verbs** (which we represent by a spring) are easiest to recognize, even though not all actions are observable.

> *We **climbed** the stairs in the Statue of Liberty.*

> *We **hope** the weather will be nice for our camping trip.*

Helping Verbs. A verb may consist of one word, as in the sentences above, or of several words. The main verb indicates the action that is taking place. The other words, called helping verbs, help to establish the **tense** of the verb, or the <u>time</u> when the action is occurring. <u>Helping verbs always come before the main verb.</u>

> *I **will see** you tomorrow.*

> *He **has read** fifteen books this year.*

> *You **should have recognized** your own picture.*

The words listed below are often used as helping verbs. Those in the first column are forms of the verb *to be*. Helping verbs are often used in combination, as you saw in the last two sentences above.

am	has	must
is	have	can
are	had	could
was	do	shall
were	does	should
be	did	will
been	may	would
	might	

<u>A word in this list is not *always* a helping verb. Sometimes it may be the main verb in a sentence.</u>

> *She **is** a doctor.*

> *I **have** five silver bracelets from Mexico.*

Linking Verbs. A linking verb does not show action. Instead it <u>links the subject of a sentence with a word in the predicate that helps to explain or describe it</u>. In this book we represent a linking verb with a chain.

> *He **is** a photographer.* (The linking verb *is* links the subject *he* with the noun *photographer. He* and *photographer* name the same person.)

> *They **were** angry.* (The linking verb *were* links the subject *they* with the adjective *angry. Angry* describes *they*.)

There are very few linking verbs. Many of them are forms of the verb *to be*, often used in combination with helping verbs.

am	has been	may be	could have been
is	have been	might be	should be
are	had been	must be	should have been
was	will be	can be	would be
were	shall be	could be	would have been

The following verbs may also be used as linking verbs. Notice that the verbs in the first column have to do with sense impressions; those in the second column have to do with how something appears; those in the third column have to do with how something is or becomes.

taste	look	become
feel	appear	grow
smell	seem	remain
sound		stay

These linking verbs may appear in various tenses, with various helping verbs.

> *The injury **sounds** serious.* (The adjective *serious* describes the subject *injury*.)

> *The milk **will become** sour if you leave it on the table.* (The adjective *sour* describes the subject *milk*.)

8

Whether these words are linking verbs or action verbs depends upon how they are used. (For a more complete explanation, see page 28.)

> *Rob **tasted** the cake.* (*Taste* is an action verb telling what Rob did.)

> *The cake **tasted** sweet.* (The cake is not doing the tasting. *Tasted* is a linking verb which links the subject *cake* with the adjective *sweet.*)

> *Ashley **looked** at the volcanic rock.* (*Looked* is an action verb telling what Ashley did.)

> *Jeff **looked** pale.* (Jeff is not doing the looking. *Looked* links the subject *Jeff* with the adjective *pale.*)

ADVERBS

An adverb is a word which <u>modifies, or describes, a verb, an adjective, or another adverb</u>. An adverb answers one of the following questions: <u>How? When? Where? How much or to what extent?</u> Because an adverb can modify so many words, answer so many questions, and appear so many places in a sentence, in this book we represent an adverb with a magic wand. Some adverbs are listed below. There are many others, however.

How? slowly, carefully, quickly, well, loudly

When? soon, now, tomorrow, often, never, seldom

Where? here, there, up, down, outside, around

How much? very, too, so, really, completely, not

Adverbs that tell *when, where,* and *how* modify verbs. Often they can work equally well in several different places in the sentence. Adverbs that tell *how much* or *to what extent* usually modify adjectives or adverbs. They are placed in front of the words they modify.

9

In the sentences below notice which words the adverbs describe and which questions they answer.

> ***Today*** *Lauren is working **very slowly**.* (*Today* modifies the verb, telling "when" Lauren is working. *Slowly* also modifies the verb, telling "how" Lauren is working. *Very* modifies the adverb *slowly,* telling "to what extent" Lauren is working slowly.)

> *Lauren is working **very slowly** today.* (Notice that the sentence works as well with *today* at the end.)

The word *not* is an adverb. Often it is placed between a helping verb and a main verb. Even when it is part of a contraction (such as *isn't*), the *n't* part of the word is an adverb.

> *I will **not** allow you to go outside today.* (*Not* modifies the verb *will allow*, telling "to what extent.")

Most words that end in an *-ly* suffix are adverbs telling "how."

PREPOSITIONS

A **preposition** <u>shows the relationship between a noun or pronoun and another word in the sentence</u>. Thinking of words that could appropriately complete the following sentence will supply you with a good list of prepositions.

> The rabbit ran _____ the yard.

Fewer than fifty words are commonly used as prepositions. Some of them are not *always* prepositions, however; their part of speech depends upon how they are used. Becoming familiar with the prepositions listed on the next page will make it easier for you to analyze sentences.

10

aboard	below	in	through
about	beneath	into	throughout
above	beside	like	to
across	between	near	toward
after	beyond	of	under
against	by	off	underneath
along	down	on	until
among	during	out	up
around	except	over	upon
at	for	past	with
before	from	since	within
behind			without

Prepositions occur in phrases called **prepositional phrases**. A prepositional phrase <u>begins with a preposition</u> and <u>ends with the object of that preposition</u>. In this book we use a magnet to represent a preposition because a preposition always needs an object. The <u>noun or pronoun</u> that is the **object** of the preposition is labeled *OP* (object of preposition) to show its function. The only words that can occur between a preposition and its object are modifying words.

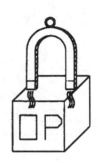

shady

> *The rabbit ran **into** the shady yard.*

From the list above, you can identify *into* as a preposition. To find the object of the preposition, ask yourself, INTO WHAT? The noun which answers that question is *yard. Shady* describes *yard.*

Prepositional phrases <u>work as either adjectives or adverbs</u>. To discover how a prepositional phrase is working, notice the kind of word it describes and the question it answers. Remember that adjectives modify nouns and pronouns, and tell *what kind, which one,* and *how many.* Adverbs modify verbs, adjectives, and adverbs, and tell *how, when, where,* and *how much* or *to what extent.*

> *The girl **with red hair** sang **at graduation**.*

With red hair tells "which" girl. Since it modifies a noun and tells "which one," the whole phrase is working as an adjective. *At grad-*

11

uation tells "where" the girl sang. Since it modifies a verb and tells "where," the whole phrase is working as an adverb.

Two or more prepositional phrases can modify the same word.

> *The store opens **at 10:00 a.m. on Saturday**.*

The phrases *at 10:00 a.m.* and *on Saturday* both modify the verb *opens*, telling "when." They are adverbial prepositional phrases.

Notice that <u>one prepositional phrase can modify the object of another prepositional phrase</u>.

> *We met **at the southwest corner of the park**.*

At the southwest corner is an adverbial prepositional phrase that modifies the verb *met* and tells "where." *Of the park* is an adjectival prepositional phrase that modifies *corner* and tells "which one."

CONJUNCTIONS

A **conjunction** is a word that <u>joins words or groups of words</u>. The most common kind of conjunction is a **coordinating conjunction**. Only the following seven words can be coordinating conjunctions.

> and   but   or   for   nor   so   yet

A coordinating conjunction may be used to join individual words, phrases, or clauses. You must be sure, however, that you use a coordinating conjunction to join the <u>same grammatical structures</u>. In this book we use glue to represent coordinating conjunctions. You would use a coordinating conjunction to join the same grammatical structures just as you might use glue to join two pieces of paper.

> *Our flag is red, white, **and** blue.* (Coordinating conjunction *and* joins adjectives in a series.)

*When we were on the camping trip, we fished for trout **and** fried our catch.* (*And* joins the verb phrases *fished for trout* and *fried our catch*.)

*Our team played hard **but** lost the game.* (The coordinating conjunction *but* joins two verb phrases *played hard* and *lost the game*.)

*Our team played hard, **but** we lost the game.* (The coordinating conjunction *but* joins two independent clauses; each could be a sentence by itself.)

Notice the following INCORRECT examples.

I like basketball, playing football, and to go swimming. (Elements in the series include a noun, a participial phrase, and an infinitive phrase. REVISION: *I like basketball, football, and swimming.*)

We'll see the movie, then we'll get a pizza.

The last sentence above contains two independent clauses; each could be a sentence by itself. Since *then* is not a coordinating conjunction, it cannot properly join these clauses. (Clauses are further discussed on pages 17 and 18.) Any of the revisions below would be CORRECT.

We'll see the movie; then we'll get a pizza.

We'll see the movie. Then we'll get a pizza.

We'll see the movie, and then we'll get a pizza.

After we see the movie, we'll get a pizza.

The last sentence above uses a **subordinating conjunction**, *after*. A subordinating conjunction <u>joins an independent clause, which can stand alone, with a dependent clause, which cannot stand alone</u>. It emphasizes the independent clause. In this book we use a screw to represent a subordinating conjunction. A subordinating conjunction joins two kinds of clauses as a screw might join metal to wood. Common subordinating conjunctions follow.

13

after	as soon as	since	whenever
although	because	so that	where
as	before	unless	wherever
as far as	even though	until	whether
as if	if	when	while

A subordinating conjunction often relates the ideas in a sentence more precisely than a coordinating conjunction can relate them. Notice that a clause containing a subordinating conjunction may come at the beginning or end of a sentence.

*The game was canceled **because** it rained.*

***Because** it rained, the game was canceled.*

Many people misuse the phrase *as far as*. Since it is a subordinating conjunction, it should introduce a *clause*, not just a noun.

INCORRECT: *As far as my homework, I finished it.*

CORRECT: ***As far as my <u>homework</u> <u>is concerned</u>,** I finished it.*

CORRECT: *As for my homework, I finished it.*

The **relative pronouns** *who, whose, whom, which, that,* and *what* work like subordinating conjunctions in that they <u>introduce dependent clauses</u>. You should use *who, whose,* and *whom* to refer to people. You should use *that* and *which* to refer to animals or things.

*The man **who** lives next door to us is an author.* (The dependent clause *who lives next door to us* interrupts the independent clause *The man is an author.*)

*Jupiter, **which** is the largest planet in the solar system, has twelve moons.* (The dependent clause *which is the largest planet in the solar system* interrupts the independent clause *Jupiter has twelve moons.*)

*Dad returned the books **that** I had read.* (The dependent clause *that I had read* follows the independent clause *Dad returned the books.*)

14

Correlative conjunctions are used in pairs.

both . . . and   either . . . or
not only . . . but also   neither . . . nor

You must be sure that the same kind of grammatical construction (word, phrase, or clause) follows each item in the pair. This is called **parallelism**. Notice the following INCORRECT example.

*We will either **go to Colorado** or **Virginia**. (Either* is followed by a verb phrase; however, its partner, *or*, is followed by a proper noun.)

Either of the following revisions would be CORRECT.

*We will go either **to Colorado** or **to Virginia**.* (Both *either* and *or* are followed by prepositional phrases.)

*We will go to either **Colorado** or **Virginia**.* (Both *either* and *or* are followed by nouns.)

INTERJECTIONS

An **interjection** has <u>no grammatical relationship</u> to the rest of the sentence. In keeping with the meaning of its word parts (*ject* meaning "throw" and *inter* meaning "between or among"), it is just "thrown into" the sentence. We use a triangular pyramid (a tetrahedron) to represent an interjection. Often an interjection is a word that expresses strong feeling and is followed by an exclamation point.

***Ouch!** I cut my finger.*

***Wow!** We won!*

Sometimes, when feeling is less strong, an interjection is followed by a comma.

***Oh**, I wondered where that pen was.*

SENTENCES

Except in informal communication, words are generally arranged in **sentences**. <u>A sentence is a group of words containing a subject and a predicate, and expressing a complete thought</u>. Knowing about sentences can help you to understand complicated sentences that you hear or read. It can also help you to use more mature sentences in your speech and writing.

SUBJECTS AND PREDICATES

The **subject** of a sentence must contain a <u>noun</u> or a <u>pronoun</u>. It <u>names something</u>. The **predicate** of a sentence contains a <u>verb</u>. It <u>tells what the subject does</u>.

> *Dogs bark.*

In the example above, the subject is *dogs*; the predicate, or verb, is *bark*. Both the subject part of a sentence and the predicate part of a sentence may include modifying words and phrases.

> **The** *dogs* **in the next yard** *bark* **loudly at night.**

Finding subjects and predicates. In analyzing a sentence, it is usually easiest to <u>find the verb, or action word, first</u>. Ask yourself what action is happening in the sentence. In the example above, the verb is *bark*.

To find the simple subject of the sentence, ask yourself, WHO BARK? The answer, of course, is *dogs*. The **simple subject** and **simple predicate** (or verb) have words describing them. All of the words and phrases describing *dogs* make up the **complete subject**; all of the words and phrases describing *bark* make up the **complete predicate**.

In the example on the next page, <u>the simple subject is underlined once, and the simple predicate is underlined twice</u>. A vertical line

16

separates the complete subject from the complete predicate. (Many grammar texts show subjects and predicates by marking sentences like this.)

*The **dogs** in the next yard* **|** *__bark__ loudly at night.*

Sometimes it is not easy to find the verb in a sentence. Perhaps the verb is a linking verb (discussed on page 8). Here are some simple ways you can check a word to see if it is a verb.

1. Is the word a linking verb or another word that is always a verb? (*is, am, are, was, were, has, have, had, should, could, would*)

2. Does the word have various forms that could be used to indicate something happening in the past, present, or future? (*walk, walked, will walk; sing, sang, sung*)

3. Can you use the word with a pronoun to indicate an action or make a statement? (*I walk; she walks; he is; they are; we sing*)

4. Can you add an *-ed* or *-ing* suffix to the word? (*be-ing, visit-ed, dream-ing*)

Not every test will work for every verb, but if the word you are testing is indeed a verb, usually at least one of the tests will work.

CLAUSES

A **clause** is a group of words containing a subject and a predicate. As you might guess, some clauses—those which express a complete thought—can stand alone as complete sentences. They are called **independent clauses**. In this book we use a block and a spring to represent an independent clause. The subject is a noun or pronoun, and the predicate is a verb. (Later we will look at independent clauses that have linking verbs.) The example sentences used so far in this Sentences section are independent clauses with action verbs.

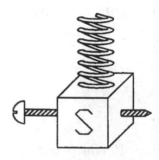

Some clauses contain a subject and verb but do not express a complete thought. They are called **dependent clauses** (or **subordinate clauses**) because they <u>cannot stand alone as complete sentences</u>. Our symbol for a dependent clause includes a block and spring (just like the independent clause). A screw has been added because the dependent clause also includes a subordinating conjunction. Just as a dependent clause does not make a complete sentence, this symbol should look incomplete to you because the screw is not attaching the block to anything.

Dependent and independent clauses can be combined to make different kinds of sentences.

SIMPLE SENTENCES

A **simple sentence** consists of just <u>one independent clause</u>, one group of words containing a subject and a predicate.

> <u>Dogs</u> <u>bark</u>.

> The **dogs** in the next yard **bark** loudly at night.

Notice that simple sentences are not necessarily short sentences. They may contain many modifiers. They are described as *simple* because they contain one clause.

COMPOUND SENTENCES

A sentence consisting of <u>two or more independent clauses</u> is called a **compound sentence**. In our model for a compound sentence you see two sym-

18

bols for independent clauses joined by glue which represents a coordinating conjunction.

In the examples below, each independent clause is enclosed in brackets. Notice that the independent clauses can be joined by a comma plus a coordinating conjunction, or by a semicolon.

[*Josh plays* soccer], *and* [*Jenny plays* golf.]

[*In May we go to Michigan*]; [*in June we go to Texas.*]

COMPOUND SUBJECTS AND VERBS

A sentence containing a compound subject or a compound verb is a simple, not a compound, sentence. It contains only one independent clause. In the sentences that follow, vertical lines separate the complete subject from the complete predicate. <u>Notice that a comma is not used between parts of a compound subject or compound verb.</u>

Rachel and *Akiko* | *are going* to the zoo.

The *girls* | *went* to the zoo and *saw* the seals.

The *men* and *women* | *sat* still and *listened* quietly to the speaker.

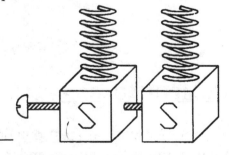

COMPLEX SENTENCES

A **complex sentence** contains <u>an independent clause and a dependent clause</u>. You see both kinds of clauses in our model.

First let's look at some dependent clauses.

*Because **we were** late.* (The dependent clause is introduced by a subordinating conjunction. See page 14 for a list of other subordinating conjunctions.)

***Which was broken**.* (The dependent clause is introduced by a relative pronoun. Other relative pronouns are *who*, *whom*, *whose*, *that*, and *what*.)

In order to make each of the preceding examples a complete sentence, an entire independent clause must be added. Notice that each independent clause could be a sentence by itself.

Dependent   **Independent**

[*Because **we were** late,*] [***we missed** our plane.*]

Independent   **Dependent**

[***This is** the vase*] [***which was broken.***]

Notice that a dependent clause can interrupt an independent clause.

[***which was broken***]
[*The **vase**   **is mended** now.*]

In the sentence above, the independent clause is *The vase is mended now.*

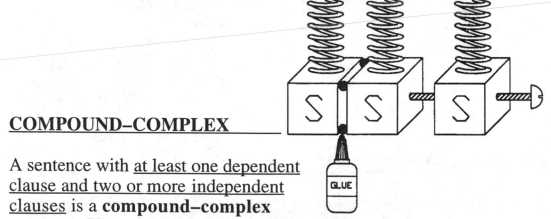

COMPOUND–COMPLEX

A sentence with <u>at least one dependent clause and two or more independent clauses</u> is a **compound–complex sentence**. You see three clauses in the model, two joined by a coordinating conjunction and the other attached with a subordinating conjunction.

> *We were planning a cruise,*   (independent clause)
>
> *but we kept it secret*   (independent clause)
>
> *until we bought our tickets.*   (dependent clause)

A compound–complex sentence may begin with the dependent clause.

SENTENCE FRAGMENTS

There are three requirements for a complete sentence: The sentence must (1) contain a subject, (2) contain a predicate, and (3) express a complete thought. If a "sentence" fails to do any one of these things, it is an <u>incomplete sentence</u>, or a **sentence fragment**. Most people use many sentence fragments in informal conversation. However, fragments should be avoided in writing and in formal situations. Here are some common errors that result in sentence fragments.

1. *The boy behind me.* (This is a subject only; it contains no predicate. It names someone but does not tell what the person did.)

2. *Dropped a tack.* (This is a predicate only; it contains no subject. It tells what happened but does not tell who performed the action. Notice that in the case of imperative sentences, or commands, discussed on page 24, subjects are not stated but are only implied. The subject is understood to be the hearer or reader of the sentence. An imperative sentence is not considered a fragment.)

3. *Missing the street sign.* (This fragment contains neither a subject nor a predicate. <u>A verb ending in *-ing* cannot be the only verb in a sentence; it needs a helping verb</u>: *She **is** missing the street sign.* Often a participial phrase such as this stands outside the independent clause of the sentence: *Missing the street sign, **she drove two blocks too far**.*)

4. *With a chip on his shoulder.* (This fragment contains neither a subject nor a predicate; it is a pair of prepositional phrases. Notice how both a subject and a predicate must be added to make a complete sentence: ***He walks** with a chip on his shoulder.*)

21

5. *When she reached the finish line.* (This is probably the most common type of sentence fragment. After all, it meets two of the three tests for a complete sentence: It contains a subject, *she*, and a verb, *reached*. However, the word *when* makes this a dependent, rather than an independent, clause. It cannot stand alone because it does not express a complete thought. It leaves a question in your mind: When she reached the finish line, what happened? To complete the sentence, an entire independent clause must be added: *When <u>she</u> <u>reached</u> the finish line, <u>**she collapsed**</u> **on the ground.**)

6. *Which I left at home.* (This is a dependent clause introduced by a relative pronoun; it must be in the same sentence as the word the relative pronoun stands for. Again, notice that an entire independent clause must be added in order to make the sentence complete: *<u>I</u> <u>**need**</u> **my clarinet**, which <u>I</u> <u>left</u> at home.*)

In general, in order to fix a fragment you need to add words, phrases, or an independent clause to make a complete sentence.

RUN-ON SENTENCES

A **run-on sentence** is the opposite of a fragment. It consists of two or more independent clauses without proper punctuation. There are three ways to correctly punctuate independent clauses.

1. *We worked all day. We played all evening.* (Clauses are punctuated as separate sentences with periods and capital letters.)

2. *We worked all day; we played all evening.* (Clauses are separated with a semicolon; a lowercase letter begins the second clause.)

3. *We worked all day, and we played all evening.* (Clauses are separated with a comma plus a coordinating conjunction.)

In each of the following INCORRECT examples, clauses are not properly separated, and a run-on sentence results.

We worked all day we played all evening.

We worked all day, we played all evening.

We worked all day, then we played all evening.

We worked all day, however we played all evening.

Notice that there are only seven coordinating conjunctions (words that can join independent clauses).

     and   but   or   for   nor   so   yet

Words such as *then*, *however*, and *therefore* require stronger punctuation.

Run-ons often occur when the second clause begins with a pronoun that refers to a noun in the first clause. Although there must be a noun for the pronoun to stand for, the noun and pronoun need not be in the same sentence.

    INCORRECT: *We were all excited about the game, it was the league championship.*

This run-on should be corrected by making separate sentences or by using a semicolon. The third method (using a comma plus a coordinating conjunction) does not work well in this case.

    CORRECT: *We were all excited about the game. It was the league championship.*

    CORRECT: *We were all excited about the game; it was the league championship.*

The following examples show you that <u>often a run-on sentence can best be fixed by relating the two ideas in some other way—by giving one idea more importance than the other</u>.

    We were all excited about the game, the league championship.

    We were all excited about the game to determine the league championship.

We were all excited about the league championship game.

We were all excited about the game because it was the league championship.

PURPOSES OF SENTENCES

Sentences may be classified according to one of four purposes. A **declarative** sentence <u>makes a statement</u>.

It is snowing outside.

Many people think Abe Lincoln was a great President.

An **interrogative** sentence <u>asks a question</u>.

Where were you when the lights went out?

An **imperative** sentence <u>makes a request or command</u>. The subject of an imperative sentence usually is not stated in the sentence. It is "understood" to be the person hearing or reading the sentence. Therefore, the subject of an imperative sentence is said to be "understood you" or "implied you." Because the subject is not stated, it is possible to have a complete imperative sentence with only one word.

Watch.

Please close the door.

Sit, Fido.

An **exclamatory** sentence <u>shows strong feeling</u>. Declarative or imperative sentences might be exclamatory.

I won the election! (declarative)

Leave me alone! (imperative)

24

SENTENCE PATTERNS

Most sentences follow one of five basic sentence patterns. Being able to identify the basic structure of a long, complicated sentence can help you understand its meaning. Models using our symbols for the parts of speech show the essential elements of these sentences.

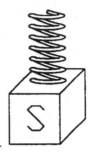

SUBJECT—VERB

The simplest of the five basic patterns is Subject–Verb (S–V). This pattern is used to tell that someone or something did something. In addition to the simple subject and action verb, the sentence may contain helping verbs, adjectives, adverbs, and prepositional phrases.

    S   **V**
Birds chirp.

    S   **V**
Birds are chirping.

           S
Two yellow birds on the branches of the pine tree

       V
have been chirping merrily this sunny morning.

As you can see from the last example above, a S–V sentence is not necessarily short. However, it would not include any of the elements named in the other patterns.

SUBJECT—LINKING VERB—PREDICATE NOUN

The second pattern consists of a subject, a linking verb, and a **predicate noun** (S–LV–PN). This pattern is used to tell who someone is or what something is. (It might be helpful to review the list of

25

linking verbs on page 8 so that you can more easily identify this pattern.) <u>Remember that the noun that follows a linking verb must name the same thing the subject names.</u> It is called a predicate noun because it is in the predicate part of the sentence. S–LV–PN sentences may also contain descriptive words and phrases.

S LV   PN
He is my father. (*He* and *father* name the same person.)

                S   **LV**
The tall man in the corner by the fireplace is my loving, generous father. (*Man* and *father* name the same person.)

<u>A predicate noun will never be part of a prepositional phrase</u>.

     S LV PN prep.   **obj.**
Second prize is a check for twenty dollars.

SUBJECT—LINKING VERB—PREDICATE ADJECTIVE

The third pattern (S–LV–PA) consists of a subject, a linking verb, and a predicate adjective. It is used to describe someone or something. The **predicate adjective**, so named because it is part of the predicate, <u>must describe the subject</u> of the sentence. Notice how this is shown in our model for this sentence pattern: The paintbrush (adjective) is joined to the block by a chain (linking verb) and is painting (or modifying) it. S–LV–PA sentences may contain other descriptive words and phrases.

S LV PA
She is tall. (*Tall* describes *she*.)

26

S
The chocolate birthday cake on the dining room table

LV   **PA**
looks indescribably delicious. (*Delicious* describes *cake*.)

Particularly notice the difference between these two sentences.

S   **LV**   **PA**
Football   is   rough.

S   **LV**   **PN**
Football   is   a   rough   sport.

Although the two sentences mean about the same thing, they follow different basic patterns. In the first sentence, the adjective *rough* describes the subject *football*; it is a predicate adjective. In the second sentence, the adjective *rough* describes the predicate noun *sport*, which names the same thing as the subject *football*. <u>You would never have a predicate noun and a predicate adjective in the same clause.</u>

Notice that sentence elements may be compound.

S   **S LV PN**
Ryan and Sean are brothers.

S LV   **PN**   **PN**
She is my neighbor and my friend.

S   **S LV PA**   **PA**
The boys and girls were hot and tired.

S   **S LV PN**   **PN**
Erin and Megan are secretary and treasurer respectively.
(The word *respectively* indicates that words are to be paired in the order named. In this case, Erin is the secretary, and Megan is the treasurer.)

27

SUBJECT—VERB—DIRECT OBJECT

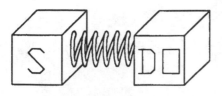 The fourth sentence pattern (S–V–DO) includes a subject, an action verb, and a **direct object**. It is used to tell that someone or something (S) is doing something (V) to someone or something else (DO). The model shows that this pattern uses an action verb rather than a linking verb.

To find the direct object in a sentence, form a question by asking, SUBJECT VERB WHAT? Notice how this works in the following sentences.

> **S   V   DO**
> *She tasted the delicious-looking cake on the dining room table.* (SHE TASTED WHAT? cake)

> **S   V   DO**
> *A small boy in a green jacket took my radio from the porch.* (BOY TOOK WHAT? radio)

> **S   V   DO   DO**
> <u>*Becky*</u> <u>*could have found*</u> *Dave and me at the mall.*
> (BECKY COULD HAVE FOUND WHOM? Dave and me)

Direct Object or Predicate Noun? Predicate nouns and predicate adjectives could also answer the question SUBJECT VERB WHAT? However, you will be able to distinguish them from direct objects if you keep these three points in mind.

1. Predicate nouns and predicate adjectives follow *linking* verbs; direct objects follow *action* verbs. Be familiar with the list of linking verbs on page 8.

2. Subjects of action verbs perform action; subjects of linking verbs do not perform action.

3. Predicate nouns or predicate adjectives must name or describe the subject of the sentence. Direct objects indicate who or what is *receiving* the action of the subject; they do not rename the subject.

                    S   V   DO
Emily decorated the cake. (Emily is doing the decorating; *Emily* and *cake* do not name the same thing.)

                    S LV   PN
Emily   is   a   cake   decorator. (Emily is not performing action; *Emily* and *decorator* name the same person.)

SUBJECT–VERB–INDIRECT OBJECT–DIRECT OBJECT

The fifth pattern (S–V–IO–DO) consists of a subject, an action verb, an **indirect object**, and a direct object. The elements are normally in this order in English. In addition to the information presented in the S–V–DO sentence, this pattern also tells to whom or for whom the action is being done. Although a sentence can include a direct object without an indirect object (S–V–DO), <u>a sentence cannot include an indirect object without also including a direct object</u>.

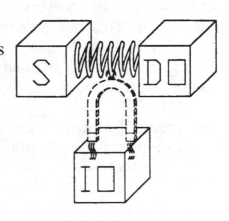

The following sequence shows the questions to ask in analyzing a sentence. First find the verb.

                V
I bought my mother a present. (To find the subject, ask WHO BOUGHT?)

        S   V
I bought my mother a present. (To find the direct object, ask I BOUGHT WHAT?)

        S   V   DO
I bought my mother a present. (To find the indirect object, ask I BOUGHT A PRESENT FOR WHOM?)

        S   V   IO   DO
I bought my mother a present.

Here are more examples of the S–V–IO–DO pattern.

$$\text{S} \quad \text{V} \quad \text{IO} \qquad \text{DO}$$
The audience gave the cast a standing ovation.

$$\text{S} \quad \text{V} \quad \text{IO} \qquad \text{DO}$$
The teacher gave us a big assignment in science.

Indirect object or object of a preposition? An indirect object is very much like a prepositional phrase with the preposition omitted. Notice that the questions used to locate indirect objects include prepositions: *To* whom? *For* whom? That is why our model for the S–V–IO–DO sentence shows the indirect object suspended from the verb by an "invisible preposition." The preposition is only implied, making an indirect object.

Compare the following pairs of sentences. The first of each pair contains a prepositional phrase, and the second contains an indirect object. The sentences in each pair have about the same meaning.

$$\text{S} \quad \text{V} \qquad \text{DO} \quad \text{prep. obj.}$$
She handed a ticket to me.

$$\text{S} \quad \text{V} \quad \text{IO} \quad \text{DO}$$
She handed me a ticket.

$$\text{S} \quad \text{V} \qquad \text{DO} \quad \text{prep. obj.}$$
I will buy a soda for you.

$$\text{S} \quad \text{V} \quad \text{IO} \quad \text{DO}$$
I will buy you a soda.

USAGE

Usage involves the way language is used in its spoken or written form. Many things affect a person's usage. For example, a three-year-old child uses language differently from the way an adult uses it. People in New England, the South, and the Midwest may choose different words and use different pronunciations. Most people use English differently in different situations. Language used in a presentation in school or on the job is likely to be different from language used in informal situations with family or friends. This section will help you know usage that will be acceptable in formal situations.

USING VERBS

Choosing the correct verb involves having the correct ending so that the verb agrees in number with its subject. Verb and subject must either both be singular or both be plural. Correct verb usage also involves choosing the correct form of an irregular verb and knowing which of two similar verbs is appropriate in a given situation.

SUBJECT–VERB AGREEMENT

For most sentences that you speak or write, subject and verb agreement will not be a problem. However, understanding the rules of subject–verb agreement will guide you through tricky situations.

1. Each noun or pronoun is either singular or plural. It is **singular** if it names <u>one</u> thing. It is **plural** if it names <u>more than one</u> thing. Most nouns form their plural by adding *s*. Notice the singular and plural forms of the following words.

Singular	book	dish	sky	child	I
Plural	books	dishes	skies	children	we

2. The subject and verb of a sentence must agree in number. That means that if the subject is singular, the verb must also be singular; if the subject is plural, the verb must also be plural. <u>Notice that an *-s* ending on a third-person verb usually indicates the *singular* form</u>.

   *The **bee buzzes**.* (singular subject and singular verb)

   *The **bees buzz**.* (plural subject and plural verb)

3. When a sentence contains a verb phrase, the *helping verb* is the part that must agree with the subject.

   *For half an hour <u>he **has been waiting**</u> for the bus.*
   (singular subject and verb *has*)

32

*For half an hour <u>they **have been waiting**</u> for the bus.*
(plural subject and verb *have*)

4. Remember that it is the *subject* that must agree in number with the verb. Prepositional phrases that come between the subject and the verb do not affect verb choice.

   A <u>**network**</u> *of nerves* <u>**carries**</u> *messages through the body.*

   The sentence may sound awkward or wrong with the singular verb *carries* directly following the plural noun *nerves*. However, the subject of the sentence—the word that must agree in number with the verb—is *network*. Both the subject and the verb are singular, and the sentence is correct.

awkward

5. These indefinite pronouns are *singular* and take singular verbs.

one	anyone	no one
each	anybody	nobody
either	everyone	someone
neither	everybody	somebody

   Everyone or *everybody* may logically seem to be plural. However, looking at the second word in these compounds may help you remember that they are singular. *Body* and *one* are obviously singular.

   <u>***Everyone***</u> <u>***likes***</u> *the new teacher.* (singular subject and verb)

   <u>***Each***</u> *of the students* <u>***has***</u> *a sack lunch.* (singular subject and verb)

6. The following indefinite pronouns are *plural* and require a plural verb.

both	few	many	several

   <u>***Few***</u> *of my friends* <u>***like***</u> *peas.* (plural subject and verb)

33

7. The following indefinite pronouns may be either singular or plural, depending on the sense of the sentence.

all   any   most   none   some

If the pronoun refers to one person or thing, it is singular and takes a singular verb. If the pronoun refers to more than one person or thing, it is plural and requires a plural verb.

All of our attention **_was focused_** on the movie. (The pronoun *all* refers to *attention*, which is singular. It requires the singular verb *was*.)

All of the students **_were awarded_** a prize. (The pronoun *all* refers to *students*, which is plural. It requires the plural verb *were*.)

Some of the excitement of being on vacation **_was lost_** after the first three days. (*Some* refers to *excitement*, which is singular.)

Some of the students **_prefer_** Sarah for class president; others prefer Andy. (*Some* refers to *students*, which is plural.)

To indicate whether they are singular or plural, the subjects of the two preceding sentences may be diagramed as shown below.

some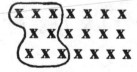

        excitement   students

        Singular   Plural

8. Subjects joined by *and* take a plural verb. (**1 + 1 = 2**)

A **_knife_** and a **_fork_** **_are used_** for cutting and eating meat. (plural)

9. Singular subjects joined by *or* or *nor* take a singular verb. **(1 or 1 = 1)**

   A __dog__ or a __cat__ __makes__ a good pet. (singular)

   Neither __Mom__ nor __Dad__ __likes__ to cook. (singular)

10. When a singular subject and a plural subject are joined by *or* or *nor*, the verb agrees with the nearer subject to make the sentence sound better.

    Neither the __teacher__ nor the __students__ __understand__ the speaker. (plural verb to agree with *students*)

    Neither the __students__ nor the __teacher__ __understands__ the speaker. (singular verb to agree with *teacher*)

11. Collective nouns (nouns that are singular in form but name a group of people or things) may be either singular or plural, depending on the meaning of the sentence. Here are examples of collective nouns.

    | audience | committee | flock | majority |
    | band | crew | group | team |
    | chorus | crowd | herd | troop |
    | class | family | jury | |

    The __jury__ __has reached__ a verdict. (*Jury* is singular because the verdict belongs to the jury as a unit.)

    The __jury__ __are arguing__ about the defendant's guilt. (*Jury* is plural because the members are being considered individually; obviously, the subject must be plural in order for arguing to occur.)

12. Words stating amounts are usually singular.

    Seventy-five __cents__ __is__ not enough money to buy lunch. (Singular subject and verb are used because *seventy-five*

35

cents is being considered as one amount, not as seventy-five separate cents.)

*Six **miles** **is** too far to run in this heat.* (singular)

13. The title of a book, organization, or country, even when plural in form, usually takes a singular verb. After all, the country, book, etc. is being considered as *one* thing.

    *The **United States** **is** my homeland.* (singular)

    ***The Twenty-One Balloons** **is** an imaginative book.*
    (singular)

14. Some nouns, although they end in *s*, are actually singular and take a singular verb. These words are examples.

civics	mathematics	mumps	physics
economics	measles	news	rickets

    *The **news** **is** on at 6:00.* (singular)

    ***Physics** **includes** the study of light, heat, sound, mechanics, and electricity.* (singular)

15. Remember that *there* and *here* can never be subjects. In a sentence beginning with one of these words, be sure to locate the subject carefully so the verb will agree with it in number. Remember, too, that *there's* and *here's*, being contractions for *there is* and *here is*, are singular. Do not use one of these contractions if your subject is plural.

    *There **are** several **reasons** why you should always fasten your seat belt.* (plural)

    *Here **are** your **ruler**, **compass**, and **protractor**.*
    (plural)

PRINCIPAL PARTS OF VERBS

The verb is the part of the sentence that indicates *when* the action of the sentence takes place—whether in the past, the present, or the future. It is important that tense be consistent in your writing. If you are telling about something that already happened, you should be writing consistently in past tense; you should not be shifting back and forth between past and present tenses.

To form the tenses you need, you must know and understand the four principal parts of each verb.

The **base word** is the simplest form of the verb. It is the form that is listed as an entry word in the dictionary. For most verbs, the **infinitive** and the **present** tense (except third person singular) are identical to the base word. The base word is used as the main verb in a present-tense sentence or in combination with helping verbs *do, does, did, may, might, must, can, could, shall, should, will,* and *would.* Often the infinitive is preceded by the word *to.* <u>An infinitive, which has no tense, can never be the main verb of a sentence.</u>

> They **check** *the temperature every morning.* (present)

> She **will check** *the depth of the water before diving.*
> (helping verb + base word = future tense)

> *Don't forget* **to check** *the roast at 6:00.* (The main verb of the "understood you" is *do forget*; *to check* is an infinitive.)

The **past** is the second principal part of the verb. It is used to tell about something that already happened. The past form is used without a helping verb.

> We **checked** *our homework in class.*

The **past participle** is the third principal part of the verb. It is used with the helping verb *have, has,* or *had* to tell about something that happened in the past, often something that continued for a while.

*She **has** already **checked** her coat.*

*We **have checked** the temperature every day this week.*

The **present participle** is the fourth principal part of the verb. It has an *-ing* ending. A present participle by itself is not enough to be the whole verb in a sentence. It must always be used with a helping verb that is some form of the verb *to be*.

*Kendra **is checking** three books out of the library.*

***Checking** his swing.* (sentence fragment)

Regular verbs form their second and third principal parts simply by adding *-ed* to the base word. (Some spelling changes may be needed as the suffix is added. For more information about spelling rules, see pages 87 through 89.)

Base Word	Past	Past Participle	Present Participle
look	looked	(have) looked	looking
save	saved	(have) saved	saving
grab	grabbed	(have) grabbed	grabbing
try	tried	(have) tried	trying

Irregular verbs form their second and third principal parts in more unusual ways, leading to most of the problems in verb usage. Tricky as these verbs are, you probably already use most of them correctly. If you memorize the principal parts of those that give you trouble, and if you understand how to form various tenses, you will improve verb usage.

Two lists of irregular verbs follow. The first is arranged alphabetically so that you can quickly check the principal parts of a particular verb. The second list groups verbs that follow a similar pattern in forming their principal parts. These words might be easier for you to remember if you study them together. The dictionary is another source for finding principal parts of verbs. Unless a verb is regular, its principal parts will be shown in a dictionary entry. Usually they will appear in boldface type near the beginning of the entry.

PRINCIPAL PARTS OF IRREGULAR VERBS
(ALPHABETICAL LIST)

Base Word	Past	Past Participle	Present Participle
beat	beat	(have) beaten	beating
become	became	(have) become	becoming
begin	began	(have) begun	beginning
bet	bet	(have) bet	betting
blow	blew	(have) blown	blowing
break	broke	(have) broken	breaking
bring	brought	(have) brought	bringing
burst	burst	(have) burst	bursting
catch	caught	(have) caught	catching
choose	chose	(have) chosen	choosing
come	came	(have) come	coming
cost	cost	(have) cost	costing
cut	cut	(have) cut	cutting
do	did	(have) done	doing
draw	drew	(have) drawn	drawing
drink	drank	(have) drunk	drinking
drive	drove	(have) driven	driving
drown	drowned	(have) drowned	drowning
eat	ate	(have) eaten	eating
fall	fell	(have) fallen	falling
fly	flew*	(have) flown	flying
freeze	froze	(have) frozen	freezing
get	got	(have) got *or* (have) gotten	getting
give	gave	(have) given	giving
go	went	(have) gone	going
grow	grew	(have) grown	growing
hang	hung**	(have) hung	hanging

---

*   Note that *flied* is correctly used in baseball terminology: *The batter **flied** out.*

** *Hang* meaning "to suspend by the neck" is a regular verb with principal parts *hang, hanged, (have) hanged, and hanging.*

Base Word	Past	Past Participle	Present Participle
hide	hid	(have) hidden	hiding
hit	hit	(have) hit	hitting
hurt	hurt	(have) hurt	hurting
know	knew	(have) known	knowing
lay	laid	(have) laid	laying
lie*	lay	(have) lain	lying
mistake	mistook	(have) mistaken	mistaking
ride	rode	(have) ridden	riding
ring	rang	(have) rung	ringing
rise	rose	(have) risen	rising
run	ran	(have) run	running
see	saw	(have) seen	seeing
set	set	(have) set	setting
shake	shook	(have) shaken	shaking
shrink	shrank *or* shrunk	(have) shrunk *or* (have) shrunken	shrinking
sing	sang	(have) sung	singing
sit	sat	(have) sat	sitting
speak	spoke	(have) spoken	speaking
spring	sprang *or* sprung	(have) sprung	springing
steal	stole	(have) stolen	stealing
stink	stank *or* stunk	(have) stunk	stinking
swim	swam	(have) swum	swimming
swing	swung	(have) swung	swinging
take	took	(have) taken	taking
teach	taught	(have) taught	teaching
throw	threw	(have) thrown	throwing
wear	wore	(have) worn	wearing
wring	wrung	(have) wrung	wringing
write	wrote	(have) written	writing

*These parts apply only to the meaning "to recline or rest." Parts of *lie* meaning "to speak falsely" are *lie*, *lied*, *(have) lied*, and *lying*.

PRINCIPAL PARTS OF IRREGULAR VERBS
(GROUPED BY PATTERN)

Base Word	Past	Past Participle
bet	bet	(have) bet
burst	burst	(have) burst
cost	cost	(have) cost
cut	cut	(have) cut
hit	hit	(have) hit
hurt	hurt	(have) hurt
set	set	(have) set
shed	shed	(have) shed
shut	shut	(have) shut
split	split	(have) split
spread	spread	(have) spread
blow	blew	(have) blown
draw	drew	(have) drawn
fly	flew	(have) flown
grow	grew	(have) grown
know	knew	(have) known
throw	threw	(have) thrown
break	broke	(have) broken
choose	chose	(have) chosen
drive	drove	(have) driven
freeze	froze	(have) frozen
ride	rode	(have) ridden
speak	spoke	(have) spoken
write	wrote	(have) written
mistake	mistook	(have) mistaken
shake	shook	(have) shaken
take	took	(have) taken
begin	began	(have) begun
drink	drank	(have) drunk
ring*	rang	(have) rung
sing	sang	(have) sung
swim	swam	(have) swum

* Note that *bring* does not follow this pattern. The past and past participle of *bring* are *brought* and *have brought*.

Base Word	Past	Past Participle
shrink	shrank *or* shrunk	(have) shrunk *or* shrunken
sink	sank *or* sunk	(have) sunk
spring	sprang *or* sprung	(have) sprung
stink	stank *or* stunk	(have) stunk
swing	swung	(have) swung
wring	wrung	(have) wrung

CONFUSING VERB PAIRS

Some verbs with similar meanings are easily confused. Three pairs are especially troublesome: *sit* and *set*, *rise* and *raise*, and *lie* and *lay*. Clearly understanding the meaning of each verb and knowing its principal parts will help you to use these words correctly.

Sit—Set

Base Word	Past	Past Participle	Present Participle
sit	sat	(have) sat	sitting
set	set	(have) set	setting

Sit means "to rest, often on the haunches." *Set* means "to put or place." *Set* is used with a direct object; *sit* is not.

Zach **sits** *near the front of the room.*

*The cat has **sat** on the windowsill each morning.*

(put)   **DO**

*Tony **set** the clean towels on the table.*

(put)   **DO**

*Mom has **set** the thermostat at 74 degrees.*

Rise—Raise

Base Word	Past	Past Participle	Present Participle
rise	rose	(have) risen	rising
raise	raised	(have) raised	raising

Both of these verbs have to do with "going up." *Rise* means "to get up" or "to go up." Something rises by itself. *Raise* means "to lift up" or "to put up." Like *set*, *raise* takes a direct object. (Notice that *raise* is a regular verb.)

*The audience **rose** when the star walked onto the stage.*

*The ash has **risen** from the volcano.*

(put up)   **DO**

*The scouts **raised** the flag at dawn.*

(lift) **DO**
Raise your hand if you agree.

Lie—Lay

Base Word	Past	Past Participle	Present Participle
lie	lay	(have) lain	lying
lay	laid	(have) laid	laying

This is probably the most confusing of all verb pairs, because the past form of *lie* is identical to the base word *lay*. Understanding the meaning of each base word and knowing the principal parts of each verb will enable you to use these words correctly.

Lie means "to recline" or "to remain in a reclining position." It is something one does to oneself. *Lay*, like *set* and *raise*, means "to put or place." *Lay* is used with a direct object. Notice that once you *lay* something down, it *lies* there.

*"**Lie** down, Fritz," Kelly commanded.*

*Yesterday I **lay** on the beach for an hour.* (past of *lie*)

*Nicole has **lain** awake for two hours.*

(put)   DO

*Please **lay** your coat on the bed.*
(present of *lay*)

(put)   DO

*Mandy has **laid** out the clothes she will wear tomorrow.*

*The coats are **lying** on the bed.*

May—Can

Both *may* and *can* are helping verbs. *May* means "to be allowed." *Can* means "to have ability."

> ***May** I go to the bathroom?*

> ***Can** you lift 300 pounds?*

Teach—Learn

Teach means "to instruct; to give knowledge or skill." *Learn* means "to receive instruction; to get knowledge or skill."

> *Mrs. Nolte **taught** us how to figure compound interest.*

> *We **learned** how to figure compound interest.*

Borrow—Lend or Loan

Borrow means "to use something temporarily with the owner's permission." *Lend* and *loan* mean "to give someone permission to use something temporarily."

> *May I **borrow** your pencil?*

> *Will you **lend** me your pencil?*

> *Will you **loan** me your pencil?*

Bring—Take

Bring means "to carry closer to the speaker." *Take* means "to carry farther away from the speaker." The correct verb, then, depends on <u>the position of the speaker in relation to the action</u>.

> *"Be sure to **bring** your science project home," Dad reminded.*

> *"Be sure to **take** your science project home," the teacher reminded.*

USING PRONOUNS

Just as a verb must agree with its subject, a pronoun must agree with the noun it stands for. Additional problems involving pronoun usage may occur in deciding whether to use a subjective or objective pronoun. Becoming familiar with the chart of pronouns on page 5 and understanding when each type of pronoun is appropriate will help you to use pronouns correctly in your speech and writing.

AGREEMENT WITH ANTECEDENT

In order for your speech or writing to be clear, a pronoun must agree with the noun it replaces. The noun and pronoun must agree in person (first, second, or third), number (singular or plural), and gender (masculine, feminine, common, or neuter). The noun usually precedes the pronoun. It is called the pronoun's **antecedent** (from the Latin words *ante*, meaning "before," and *cede*, meaning "go").

> *Asha rode **her** bicycle to school. (Her* refers to *Asha*—third person, singular, feminine.)

> *Mike and Lindsey left **their** project at home. (Their* refers to *Mike and Lindsey*—third person, plural, common.)

> *Many trees shed **their** leaves in autumn. (Their* refers to *trees*—third person, plural, neuter.)

Agreement between a pronoun and its antecedent is most likely to become a problem when indefinite pronouns are used. Study the lists on page 33 to determine which indefinite pronouns are singular and which are plural. Remember that words such as *everyone* and *everybody* are singular and, therefore, require singular pronouns.

> *Everyone forgot **his** lunch. (His* refers to *everyone*—third person singular.)

Until recently, *his* was widely accepted to refer to all people, both masculine and feminine, in such situations. Today many people believe that a feminine pronoun should be used half the time. This can result in an awkward alternating between masculine and feminine throughout a piece of writing, or in the cumbersome repetition of "his and her," "she and he," etc. Since English has no third person singular pronoun of common gender, there is no clear solution to this dilemma. Sometimes people try to solve the problem by substituting *their* for *his: Everyone forgot their lunch.* Although the problem of gender is solved, these pronouns do not agree in number, since *everyone* is singular and *their* is plural. Often the best solution is to make the sentence plural: *All of the people forgot their lunches.*

SUBJECTIVE PRONOUNS

Subjective pronouns (often called nominative pronouns) are used as the subject of a sentence and after a linking verb.

They cleaned up the litter along the highway.

It was *I* who discovered the clue.

Who saw you at the mall?

You are most likely to have a problem with subjective pronouns when you have a compound subject. To decide if a pronoun is correct, try using it as the only subject of the sentence.

> *She* and *I* enjoyed the play. (Out of courtesy, first person is listed last.)

> *She* enjoyed the play. (NOT *Her* enjoyed the play.)

> *I* enjoyed the play. (NOT *Me* enjoyed the play.)

Note that in third person present tense you will need a different verb form as you change from plural to singular to test your pronoun.

> *He* and *Adam* *play* soccer.

> *He* *plays* soccer. (NOT *Him* plays soccer.)

If a noun referring to the same person or thing immediately follows the pronoun, drop the noun to test for correct pronoun usage.

> *We* *girls* practice field hockey every day after school.

> *We* practice field hockey every day after school.
> (NOT *Us* practice field hockey every day after school.)

Although a phrase such as *we girls* is acceptable for emphasis or clarification, <u>a pronoun should not be used immediately *after* a noun subject</u>. Use either the noun or the pronoun.

> NONSTANDARD: *My* *brother* *he* taught me to juggle.

> STANDARD: *My* *brother* taught me to juggle.

> STANDARD: *He* taught me to juggle.

OBJECTIVE PRONOUNS

Objective pronouns are used as direct objects, indirect objects, and objects of prepositions.

*We found **him** hiding behind a tree.* (direct object)

*She brought **us** coins from India.* (indirect object)

*Mrs. Lopez showed the bones to **them**.* (object of preposition)

*To **whom** is the letter addressed?* (object of preposition)

***Whom** did you see at the mall?* (direct object; question affects normal word order)

Once again, compound situations are most likely to cause problems. Considering each part of the compound object individually can help you to choose the correct pronoun.

*Ms. Schaffer asked **him** and **me** to water the plants.*
(Out of courtesy, first person is listed last.)

*Ms. Schaffer asked **him** to water the plants.*
(NOT *Ms. Schaffer asked **he** to water the plants.*)

*Ms. Schaffer asked **me** to water the plants.*
(NOT *Ms. Schaffer asked **I** to water the plants.*)

*Mr. Lee read **us** and **them** a story.*

*Mr. Lee read **us** a story.* (NOT *Mr. Lee read **we** a story.*)

*Mr. Lee read **them** a story.* (NOT *Mr. Lee read **they** a story.*)

Dropping the noun immediately following a pronoun that refers to the same thing is an effective test for correct pronoun usage.

49

*It was a secret just between **us girls**.*

*It was a secret just between **us**.*

Notice that you would <u>never use a subjective pronoun and an objective pronoun together in a compound</u>.

NONSTANDARD: ***Him and I** went to the party.* (The pronouns are the subjects of the sentence. *I* is a subject pronoun, but *him* is not.)

STANDARD: ***He and I** went to the party.* (Both pronouns are correctly used as subjects.)

NONSTANDARD: *The letter was for **her and I**.* (The pronouns *her* and *I* are used as objects of the preposition *for*. *Her* can be an object, but *I* cannot.)

STANDARD: *The letter was for **her and me**.* (Both pronouns are correctly used as objects.)

PRONOUNS IN INCOMPLETE COMPARISONS

Sometimes pronouns are used in comparisons that are not completely stated. In order to choose the correct pronoun, you must be able to supply the implied words and notice whether the pronoun is used as a subject or an object.

*Shelly is taller than **I** [am tall]. (I is a subject.)*

*Tim likes Ben more than **I** [like Ben]. (I is a subject.)*

*Tim likes Ben more than [he likes] **me**. (Me is used as a direct object. Compare this example with the previous one to notice how the choice of pronoun completely changes the meaning of the sentence.)*

USING MODIFIERS

Modifiers are words that describe. To use modifiers correctly, you must be sure that you use the right part of speech as well as the right form of the modifier. Placing the modifier as close as possible to the word it describes usually helps to make your writing clearer.

ADJECTIVE OR ADVERB?

Sometimes an adjective is incorrectly used as an adverb. Remember that an adjective describes a noun or a pronoun, and tells "what kind," "which one," or "how many." An adverb describes a verb, an adjective, or another adverb, and tells "when," "where," "how," "how much," or "to what extent."

Many adverbs are formed by adding the *-ly* suffix to adjectives.

Adjectives (Describe Nouns)	Adverbs (Describe Verbs)
careful (driver)	(drive) carefully
harsh (words)	(speak) harshly
easy (job)	(complete) easily
lazy (person)	(lounge) lazily

A few short words, such as *soft*, *loud*, *quick*, and *slow*, can be used as either adjectives or adverbs. These words also have other adverb forms that have the *-ly* suffix: *softly, loudly, quickly, slowly*. The adverb form having the suffix is usually used in formal situations.

Good—Well

Probably the adjective–adverb pair causing greatest confusion is *good* and *well*. *Good* is an adjective; *well* is usually an adverb.

> *She did a **good** job on her math test.* (*Good* describes the noun *job*, telling "what kind" of job.)

> *She did **well** on her math test.* (*Well* tells "how" she did, describing the verb.)

Good should be used after a linking verb. (See page 8.)

> *The soup smells* **good**. (*Good* describes the noun *soup*.)

> *The news is* **good**. (*Good* describes the noun *news*.)

> *Well* meaning "in good health" is an adjective.

> *I don't feel* **well**. (*Well* describes the pronoun *I*.)

COMPARISON OF ADJECTIVES

Adjectives have three forms: positive, comparative, and superlative. Understanding these forms will help you to use modifiers correctly.

The **positive** form is used if only one thing is being described.

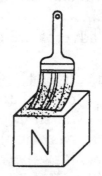

> *Luis is a* **kind** *boy.*

The **comparative** form is used to compare two people or things.

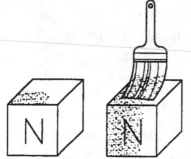

> *Luis is* **kinder** *than Kevin.*

> *Of the two boys, who is* **kinder**?

> *Luis is* **kinder** *than anyone else in the class.* (At first this might appear to be a comparison involving more than two people. However, *anyone* is singular; Luis is being compared with only one person at a time.)

The **superlative** form is used if more than two people or things are being compared.

*Luis is the **kindest** boy
in the class.*

*Of all the boys, Luis is
the **kindest**.*

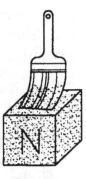

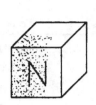

The preceding examples show the most common way of comparing adjectives: *-er* is added to the positive to form the comparative, and *-est* is added to the positive to form the superlative. Adding these suffixes sometimes requires simple spelling changes. See pages 87 through 89 for more information about spelling rules.

Some words, particularly those of more than two syllables, would become awkward to pronounce if these suffixes were added. Instead, longer words (and even a few two-syllable words) substitute the word *more* for the *-er* suffix and the word *most* for the *-est* suffix.

The following chart compares a variety of adjectives. Since there are thousands of adjectives, this list merely provides examples.

Positive	Comparative	Superlative
clean	cleaner	cleanest
bold	bolder	boldest
white	whiter	whitest
sad	sadder	saddest
pretty	prettier	prettiest
wealthy	wealthier	wealthiest
useful	more useful	most useful
famous	more famous	most famous
beautiful	more beautiful	most beautiful
valuable	more valuable	most valuable

<u>The *-er* or *-est* suffix is never used with *more* or *most*; one or the other is used.</u> In other words, a comparison such as *more taller* would be nonstandard. In addition, notice that if a suffix is used to form the comparative, a suffix is also used to form the superlative. If *more* is used to form the comparative, *most* is used to form the superlative.

A few adjectives change their form completely when they are compared. Such irregular forms can be found in the dictionary entry for the positive form of the word.

Positive	Comparative	Superlative
good	better	best
bad	worse	worst
many	more	most
much	more	most
few	fewer	fewest
little*	less *or* lesser	least
far	farther *or* further	farthest *or* furthest

*This comparison is used for *little* meaning "small amount." *Little* meaning "small in size" would be regularly compared.

These irregularly compared adjectives can cause special problems. *Many* and *few* are used to describe plural things. *Much* and *little* are used to describe singular things of which a part is considered.

> *I have **many assignments** to complete tonight.* (*Many* describes the plural noun *assignments*.)

> *I have **much homework** to complete tonight.* (*Much* describes the singular noun *homework*.)

> ***Few thunderstorms** occur in the desert.* (*Few* describes the plural noun *thunderstorms*.)

> ***Little rain** falls in the desert.* (*Little* describes the singular noun *rain*.)

The words *less* and *least* are used to show a negative comparison.

> *Kevin is **less kind** than Luis.*

Particularly troublesome are the comparative adjectives *fewer* and *less*. *Fewer* should be used to describe plural things; *less* should be used to describe singular things.

Fewer people than we expected attended the program. (*Fewer* describes the plural noun *people*.)

*Because we had a snack after school, there were **fewer grapes** for dinner than we wanted.* (*Fewer* describes the plural noun *grapes*.)

*Because we had a snack after school, there was **less fruit** for dinner than we wanted.* (*Less* describes the singular noun *fruit*.)

*Because of the drought, there is **less water** in the river than usual.* (*Less* describes the singular noun *water*.)

Notice that some adjectives have no comparative form because the qualities they describe do not exist in degrees.

     perfect   dead   square   round   unique

Something is either perfect or it isn't; it can't be *more perfect* or *less perfect*. The phrases *nearly perfect* and *more nearly perfect* may be used, however, to describe something approaching perfection.

COMPARISON OF ADVERBS

Like adjectives, adverbs have three forms: positive, comparative, and superlative. The positive form is used to describe one action.

*Melissa works **fast**.*

The comparative form is used to compare two actions.

*Melissa works **faster** than Stephanie [works].*

The superlative form is used to compare more than two actions.

*Of all students in her group, Melissa works **fastest**.*

The comparative form of some adverbs is made by adding *-er*, and the superlative form of those same adverbs is formed by adding *-est*. However, many adverbs already have an *-ly* suffix; adding an additional suffix would make them awkward to pronounce. Therefore, the comparative and superlative forms of most adverbs use the words *more* (or *less*) and *most* (or *least*).

The following chart compares a variety of adverbs.

Positive	Comparative	Superlative
slow	slower	slowest
slowly	more slowly	most slowly
early	earlier	earliest
noisily	more noisily	most noisily
gracefully	more gracefully	most gracefully
well	better	best

MAKING COMPARISONS LOGICAL

When making a comparison, be sure you are comparing the things you mean to compare.

ILLOGICAL: *Is television advertising more effective than radio?* (The two elements being compared here are *television advertising* and *radio*. Although *radio* can be compared with *television*, it cannot logically be compared with *television advertising*.)

LOGICAL: *Is television advertising more effective than radio advertising? (Television advertising* is compared with *radio advertising*.)

LOGICAL: *Is advertising on television more effective than advertising on radio?*

Avoid the following additional kind of illogical comparison.

ILLOGICAL: *Matt is neater than anyone in the class.* (If Matt is a member of the class, he cannot possibly be neater than himself.)

LOGICAL: *Matt is neater than anyone **else** in the class.*

ILLOGICAL: *Aleta likes the giraffe better than any animal.* (Obviously, the giraffe itself is an animal.)

LOGICAL: *Aleta likes the giraffe better than any **other** animal.*

DOUBLE NEGATIVES

In math you learned that two negatives often make a positive. This is also true in language.

Nobody *doesn't like Sara Lee.*

The two negatives (*nobody* and *n't* in *doesn't*) make a positive. The writers of this familiar slogan discovered a clever, memorable way to express the idea that everyone *does* like their product. What they really mean is *Everybody **does** like Sara Lee.*

Sometimes people use two negatives in everyday speaking or writing, perhaps intending to emphasize their negative idea. In fact, use of the double negative reveals a lack of standard usage in addition to misleading the audience.

The following words are negative. You should use only one of them (not two) to express a negative idea.

no	never	nothing
not (n't)	no one	hardly
none	nobody	scarcely

NONSTANDARD:	*I don't have **no** money.* (two negatives)
STANDARD:	*I don't have any money.* (one negative)
STANDARD:	*I have **no** money.* (one negative)

NONSTANDARD:	*She **never** does **nothing** to help me.* (two negatives)
STANDARD:	*She **never** does anything to help me.* (one negative)

NONSTANDARD:	*I couldn't **hardly** hear him.* (two negatives)
STANDARD:	*I could **hardly** hear him.* (one negative)

SPECIAL SITUATIONS WITH MODIFIERS

A few modifiers may require special attention in order to be used correctly.

A—An

Use *a* before a word beginning with a consonant sound and *an* before a word beginning with a vowel sound. This makes the words easier to pronounce.

> *Steve had **an o**range and **a b**anana for lunch.*

> *We played hockey for **an** hour.* (Although *hour* starts with a consonant, the *h* is silent. *An* is used because *hour* starts with a vowel *sound*.)

This—That—These—Those

In using these adjectives, remember that *this* and *that* are singular; *these* and *those* are plural. In addition, *this* and *these* refer to objects nearby; *that* and *those* refer to things farther away. The meanings of the adjectives themselves already give information about the location of the noun described. Therefore, it is unnecessary (and nonstandard) to use *this here* and *that there*.

*The notebook on **this** desk is mine.* (one desk nearby)

*The notebook on **that** desk is yours.* (one desk far away)

(near—plural)   (far—plural)
***These** flowers look fresher than **those** flowers.*

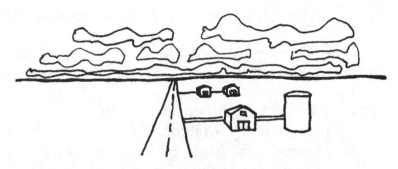

***This** farm has a grain bin; **that** farm does not.*

Errors often occur when the noun modified is *kind* or *sort*. When one of these nouns is singular, it must be preceded by a singular adjective, regardless of other plural words that may be included in the sentence.

*I have never seen **this kind** of vase before.* (singular)

***Those kinds** of animals belong in the zoo.* (plural)

Remember that the word *them* is an objective pronoun, not an adjective. It should be used to replace a noun, not to describe a noun.

NONSTANDARD: ***Them** colored pencils are mine.*

STANDARD: ***Those** colored pencils are mine; I bought **them** yesterday.*

POSITION OF MODIFIERS

In order to make your communication clear, place modifying words and phrases as close as possible to the words they modify. Notice, for example, how the meaning of a sentence changes completely as *only* is moved to different positions.

>He **only seemed** interested in science. (He wasn't really interested.)

>He seemed interested **only in science**. (He didn't seem interested in anything else.)

>**Only he** seemed interested in science. (No one else did.)

Misplaced phrases may result in humorous, misleading sentences.

>MISLEADING: *The fire was put out before any damage was done **by the local fire department**.* (Since *by the local fire department* modifies *was put out*, it should be placed closer to that phrase.)

>CLEAR: *The fire was put out **by the local fire department** before any damage was done.*

>MISLEADING: *I saw an **owl walking home from school**.* (Since the phrase follows *owl*, it sounds like the owl is walking.)

>CLEAR: ***Walking home from school**, I saw an owl.* (The participial phrase is now next to the word it describes.)

A participial phrase (either present or past) that begins a sentence should modify the subject of that sentence.

>MISLEADING: ***Giggling uncontrollably**, the elevator took us to the sixth floor.* (The participial

60

phrase *giggling uncontrollably* should modify the subject, which is *elevator*. Since elevators cannot giggle, the sentence should be revised.)

CLEAR: ***Giggling uncontrollably, we** took the elevator to the sixth floor.* (The subject was changed to be the word modified by the participial phrase.)

CLEAR: *While **we were giggling** uncontrollably, the elevator took us to the sixth floor.* (The participial phrase was expanded to a full clause with a subject of its own.)

MISLEADING: ***Disappointed and exhausted, the bus** carried us home from the game.* (The past participles, *disappointed* and *exhausted*, should modify the subject, *bus*. Since this is illogical, the sentence should be revised.)

CLEAR: ***Disappointed and exhausted, we** rode the bus home from the game.* (The subject was changed to be the word modified by the participial phrase.)

CLEAR: ***We were** disappointed and exhausted as the bus carried us home from the game.* (The participial phrase was expanded to a clause with a subject of its own.)

61

MECHANICS

Mechanics involves the nitty-gritty details of written language: capitalization, punctuation, and spelling. If attention is not paid to these details, meaning can be difficult—or even impossible—to figure out. Although the following paragraph contains no misspelled words, it has no punctuation or capitalization. See if you can find two completely different ways to punctuate the paragraph. They will result in two completely different meanings. (Remember that sentences do not need to start with the subject.)

Memorable Students

they are the memorable students in any class they participate fully in any mischief they see no point in volunteering for extra jobs they delight in distracting their classmates they take no pleasure in learning they are never satisfied

---

Knowing the rules of mechanics will help you to understand what you read. Applying those rules in your own writing will help you communicate your message to others.

CAPITALIZATION

In general, words that are capitalized are proper nouns—words that name <u>particular</u> people, places, things, or ideas.

1. Capitalize the names and initials of people and pets. Titles, such as *Mr.*, *Miss*, and *Dr.*, are also capitalized. Names of relatives are capitalized when they are used as *names*. If they are simply used as words and are preceded by modifiers such as *a*, *this*, or *my*, they are lower-cased.

   Shannon studied music with
   Dr. Scott E. Bauer.

   *We left our bird, **Bangles**, with **Aunt Carol** while we visited **our grandma**.*

2. Always capitalize the word *I*. (Be sure you do not get into the habit of capitalizing other short words, such as *is* and *it*, that also begin with *i*.)

   *On our trip **I** navigated for Mom, who drove the car.*

3. Capitalize the first letter of each sentence.

4. Capitalize names of days of the week, months of the year, and holidays. Do *not* capitalize the names of seasons.

   *This year **Labor Day** is on **Monday**, September 7.*

   *I like the pastel flowers of **spring** and the crimson leaves of **autumn**.*

September						
S	M	T	W	Th	F	S
		1	2	3	4	5
6	Labor Day 7	8	9	10	11	12
13	14	15	16	17	18	19
20	21	22	23	24	25	26
27	28	29	30			

5. Capitalize names of towns, cities, states, countries, planets, galaxies, etc. The word *earth* is capitalized only when it refers to our planet and is not preceded by a modifier, such as *the* or *our*.

The word *moon* is not capitalized, because it is a common noun rather than a proper noun.

*My family used to live in **Miami**, **Florida**.*

*Astronauts went from the **earth** to the **moon** and back.*

*__Venus__ and **Earth** are known as twin planets.*

6. Capitalize the names of streets, mountains, and bodies of water. Notice that most of these names contain more than one word. <u>Be sure to capitalize all words in the name</u>.

*Union Station is located on **Market Street**.*

*We flew over the **Rocky Mountains** and the **Great Salt Lake**.*

7. Capitalize names of businesses, organizations, governmental bodies, and buildings.

*The new product manufactured by **Monsanto** has been approved by the **Food and Drug Administration**.*

*Our **Girl Scout** troop went to the top of the **Gateway Arch**.*

*The **Senate** and the **House of Representatives** make up **Congress**.*

8. Capitalize words that refer to God, religions, denominations, and religious books. The word *god* is capitalized only when it refers to the Supreme Being.

*The sacred scripture of **Islam** is the **Koran**.*

Methodists, *Presbyterians*, *Roman Catholics*, *and Baptists* all believe in the *Bible*.

The ancient Greeks believed in many **gods**, *the most powerful of whom was* **Zeus**.

9. Capitalize proper adjectives made from proper nouns.

> *American*, *European*, *African*, *Asian*, *and Australian* *athletes compete in the Olympic games.*

> *We ordered* **French** *toast for breakfast and* **Spanish** *rice for dinner.*

10. Capitalize words that refer to particular groups of people, such as tribes or races. (When the word *black* or *white* is used to refer to race, it generally is not capitalized.) The word *Indian* is always capitalized, whether it refers to a Native American or to someone from the country of India.

> *The* **Navajo** *and* **Apache Indians** *made their home in the southwestern United States.*

> *The first* **Negroes** *were brought to the United States in 1619.*

> *Rosa Parks was one of the modern leaders in obtaining rights for* **blacks**.

11. Capitalize names of historical events, periods, documents, and prizes.

> *The period of rebuilding the South after the* **Civil War** *was called* **Reconstruction.**

> *The* **Declaration of Independence** *is on display in Washington, D.C.*

> *Will an American win a* **Nobel Prize** *this year?*

12. Capitalize names of vehicles—ships, planes, spacecraft, cars, trains, etc. (Names of particular vehicles—but not types of vehicles—should also be italicized or underlined.)

Charles Lindbergh flew from New York to Paris in the **Spirit of St. Louis***.*

According to legend, Casey Jones died trying to bring the **Cannonball** *in on time.*

The **Toyota Corolla** *is a popular import.*

13. Capitalize trade names but not the common nouns indicating the type of product.

A commercial for **Irish Spring soap** *shows suds coming out of a person's clothes.*

I bleached my **Levi jacket** *in* **Clorox***.*

14. Capitalize titles when they are used with a name or in place of a name. Do not capitalize these words if they are used as common nouns. (An exception to this is the noun *president*, which is capitalized if it refers to the President of the United States.) Also capitalize the abbreviation of a degree following a person's name.

Mayor *Rolla Wells helped to bring the World's Fair to St. Louis in 1904.*

What is your opinion of the new ordinance, **Mayor***?*

We visited **the mayor's office** *on our field trip.*

Who will be the next **President** *of the United States?*

The black bag belongs to Lisa Collins, **M.D.**

15. Capitalize abbreviations of words that would be capitalized. Do not capitalize abbreviations of words that would not be capitalized. (Few abbreviations are acceptable in formal writing.)

> The **U.S.** Department of Agriculture provides assistance to farmers.

> A person's normal body temperature is 98.6 degrees **F.**

> *6 ft. 4 in.*

16. Capitalize direction words only if they designate geographic regions. Do not capitalize them if they merely indicate direction.

> The **Middle East** has been an area of unrest for thousands of years.

> The **South** is becoming more industrialized.

> We traveled **west** for 2,000 miles to get to California.

17. Do not capitalize school subjects unless they name languages or particular numbered courses (as in college).

> We study **math**, **science**, **social studies**, **English**, **music**, **art**, and **German**.

> According to my placement test, I should register for **Math 186**.

18. Capitalize the first letter of a direct quotation. Do not capitalize the first letter of a continuing quotation when the tag (the words identifying the speaker) occurs in the middle of a sentence. (For information about punctuating direct quotations, see pages 80 through 82.)

> Jessica asked, "**Where** are my blue socks?"

> "**Where**," Jessica asked, "**are** my blue socks?"

67

19. In titles of books, poems, songs, stories, etc., capitalize the first letter of the first word, the last word, and all other important words. Verbs and pronouns are usually considered to be important words. Words that are not considered important are articles (*a*, *an*, and *the*), coordinating conjunctions (*and*, *but*, *or*, etc.), and prepositions of fewer than five letters. (For more information about setting off titles, see pages 82 and 83.)

> *The guest of honor was reunited with people he or she hadn't seen in years on **This Is Your Life**.*

> *Everyone stood to sing **"The Star-Spangled Banner"** before the ball game began.*

> ***Around the World in Eighty Days*** *is a fascinating book by Jules Verne.*

20. Capitalize the first word and the name in the salutation of a letter and the first word only of the closing.

> **Dear Grandpa**,

>> **Your** *nephew,*

> **Dear Ms. Tanaka**:

>> **Yours** *truly,*

21. In outlines, capitalize the first word of each main head and sub-head. (For information on outline form see pages 115 and 116.)

22. Capitalize the first word of each line of poetry. (Many modern poems do not follow this traditional form.)

> **Quietly** *I watched the rain*
> **Trickle** *down the window pane.*

PUNCTUATION

One definition of *punctuate* is "to interrupt at intervals." Stars "punctuate" the night sky or cheers may "punctuate" a speech, calling attention to certain ideas. In the same way, punctuation marks break up a block of writing, making it easier to understand.

All punctuation marks except opening quotation marks, opening parentheses, and opening brackets directly follow a word (without a space between the word and the punctuation mark). Therefore, they <u>should never be used at the beginning of a line of writing</u>.

PERIOD ●

1. Use a period at the end of a declarative or imperative sentence.

    Today is a very warm day. (declarative)

    Please open the window. (imperative)

    Some sentences involving speculation are really declarative or imperative, requiring a period rather than a question mark.

    I wonder what time it is. (declarative)

    Guess how much this costs. (imperative)

    People sometimes use question form for requests to which they do not expect a spoken reply. This kind of request should be followed by a period rather than a question mark.

    Will the audience please stand.

2. Use a period after an abbreviation or an initial. Never use more than one period at the end of a sentence.

    *Our next-door neighbor is **R. W. Garcia, M.D.***

69

The United States Postal Service prefers that everyone use two-letter state abbreviations in addresses. Both letters of these abbreviations are capitalized, and no periods are used. In sentences, however, the names of states are generally spelled out.

MN = Minnesota   **ME** = Maine

QUESTION MARK   ?

Use a question mark at the end of an interrogative sentence.

What time is it?

Some sentences have the grammatical form of a statement, but the way they are spoken (or intended to be read) indicates that they are questions. A question mark should be used after such a sentence.

You found your science book in the refrigerator?

On the other hand, some requests have the grammatical form of a question even though no spoken reply is expected. This kind of request should be followed by a period.

Will you please return the form as soon as possible.

Some sentences involving uncertainty are really declarative or imperative rather than interrogative. They require a period rather than a question mark.

I wonder how many stars are in the sky. (declarative)

Guess how many beans are in the jar. (imperative)

EXCLAMATION POINT

1. Use an exclamation point at the end of a sentence that shows surprise or strong feeling. (Note that the form of the sentence may be declarative or imperative.)

   What an exciting game it was! (exclamatory)

   It's snowing! (declarative)

   Watch out for that hole in the ground! (imperative)

2. Use an exclamation point after an interjection that shows strong feeling.

   Ouch! You stepped on my toe.

COMMA

A comma is used to separate various kinds of information within a sentence. Words that are closely related, such as subject and verb, adjective and noun, and preposition and object, generally will not be separated by a comma. Separating the various elements helps to make the independent clause stand out for the reader so that the main idea of the sentence is easier to find and understand.

If you know the reasons for using commas, you will more easily understand what you read, and other people will more easily understand what you write. Simply putting a comma "where you would pause" is not a reliable guide for punctuating sentences.

1. Use a comma to separate the name of a city or town from the name of a state or country. If this appears in the middle of a sentence, use a comma after the state or country also.

   *We went to **Chicago, Illinois**, to see the museums.*

71

Do not use any punctuation between the state and the ZIP code.

Boise, ID 83708

2. Use a comma to separate the day of the month from the year. If this appears in the middle of a sentence, use a comma after the year also.

    On **July 20, 1969,** *the first person landed on the moon.*

3. Use a comma after the salutation (or greeting) of a friendly letter.

    Dear Heather,

4. Use a comma after the closing of any letter.

    Your friend,

5. Use a comma after a last name which precedes a first name, as on a form or in a list.

    Henderson, Susan E.

6. In a series of three or more items, use a comma after each item except the last. Do not use a comma before the first item.

    *She needed **a hammer, a nail, and a screwdriver** in order to hang the towel rack.*

    If a series is preceded by *such as*, use a comma before *such* and after the last item in the series. In the example below, notice that the sentence would be complete and would give the same basic message if the entire boldface section were omitted.

    *Basic tools, **such as a hammer, a screwdriver, and a wrench,** are essential in any home.*

7. If two or more adjectives describe the same noun and they could appropriately be connected with *and*, use a comma between them.

> The **small, furry kitten** huddled in the corner.

> The **large delivery truck** blocked the street. (No comma is used because you wouldn't say *large and delivery truck*. *Large* describes *delivery truck*, not just *truck*.)

8. Use a comma before the conjunction in a compound sentence (*and, but, or, nor, for, so,* or *yet*).

> He wanted to see the show, **but** he had band practice at the same time.

Note that a comma is not used if only the verb is compound.

> He **wanted** to see the show but **had** band practice at the same time.

9. Use a comma to separate a direct quotation from its tag (the words that identify the speaker).

> **Alicia asked,** "What seems to be the problem?"

> "What," **Alicia asked,** "seems to be the problem?"

If the tag follows a quotation that is a question or an exclamation, a question mark or exclamation point is used instead of a comma.

> "What seems to be the problem?" **Alicia asked.**

10. Use a comma after an introductory word, such as *yes, no, well,* or *oh*.

> **Yes,** I would love to go to the wolf howl tonight.

11. Use one or two commas to set off an expression that interrupts a sentence or is not part of the independent clause. Examples of such expressions are *too, of course, however, for example, by the way, on the other hand, in my opinion, don't you,* and *nevertheless.*

> He would like to visit Hawaii, **too**.

> He, **too**, would like to visit Hawaii.

> You realize, **of course**, that I'm kidding.

> I enjoy water skiing, **don't you**?

Be sure to use stronger punctuation (a period or semicolon) if the expression comes *between* clauses rather than within a clause.

> <u>We</u> <u>tried</u> to lift the rock**; however,** <u>it</u> <u>would</u> not <u>budge</u>. (With two clauses, this is a compound sentence. If the semicolon were replaced with a comma, it would be a run-on.)

> We pulled up the small tree. The <u>rock</u>**, however,** <u>would</u> not <u>budge</u>. (*However* comes in the middle of a clause and simply needs to be set off by commas.)

12. Use one or two commas to set off the <u>name of a person spoken to</u>. This is called **direct address**. Notice that each of these sentences would be complete if the name were omitted.

> **Jason,** could you please help me?

> If you wait, **Amber,** I'll go with you.

> What do you want, **Mother**?

13. Use one or two commas to set off an **appositive** (a noun or noun phrase that names the same thing as a noun or noun phrase right next to it in the sentence).

Chris, my best friend, lives next door to me. (*Chris* and *my best friend* name the same person.)

Notice that the sentence would be complete if the appositive were omitted; the reader simply would not have as much information.

14. Prepositional phrases are generally not set off by commas. However, a long introductory prepositional phrase or series of phrases may be followed by a comma.

> *In the deepest recess of the cave, the bear slept for the winter.*

You should definitely use a comma if it is necessary to prevent misreading.

LIKELY TO BE MISREAD: *In the summer days seem to pass quickly.* (On first reading it is unclear whether *summer* is a noun or an adjective.)

REVISED FOR CLARITY: *In the summer, days seem to pass quickly.* (The comma clarifies that *summer* is the object of the preposition *in*.)

15. Use a comma after a dependent clause at the beginning of a sentence. (For a list of subordinating conjunctions, which often begin dependent clauses, see page 14.)

> *As the car sped away, the witness quickly jotted down the license number.*

A dependent clause at the end of a sentence is usually not set off by a comma. A comma may be used, however, if information in the dependent clause contrasts strongly with information presented earlier in the sentence.

*The witness quickly jotted down the license number **as the car sped away**.*

*I will go along with your plan, **although I will be surprised if it works**.*

16. Use a comma to set off adjectives or other elements that follow the main clause of a sentence.

    *Under the porch we found the puppy, **cold and whimpering**.*

    *The store has many items on sale, **such as jeans, sweatshirts, and sweaters**.*

17. Use a comma to separate a **non-restrictive participial phrase** or **absolute phrase** from the rest of a sentence. These phrases contain information that is <u>not essential</u> to the meaning of the sentence.

    ***Frightened by the gunshot,** the horse reared, **throwing its rider to the ground**.* (past and present participial phrases)

    ***His eyes focused on the TV,** he pretended not to hear her.* (absolute phrase)

    Each sentence would be complete without the non-restrictive phrase; it just would not be as descriptive. A comma in this type of sentence helps to set off the independent clause, the part of the sentence that contains the most important information.

18. Use a comma to set off a **non-restrictive clause**. A non-restrictive clause is one that provides <u>extra information</u>.

*Saturn, **which is the sixth planet from the sun,** is known for its rings.*

In the sentence above, removing the clause set off by commas would not change the basic meaning of the sentence; the reader would simply be missing one piece of information.

A **restrictive** clause—one that is <u>necessary</u> to the meaning of the sentence—should not be set off by commas.

*Meat **which has been left unrefrigerated for several days** is unfit to eat.*

The boldface clause is restrictive. It is necessary to explain (or restrict) which meat is meant. Eliminating the restrictive clause completely changes the meaning of the sentence and results in an untrue statement (*Meat is unfit to eat*).

SEMICOLON ;

A semicolon provides punctuation that is stronger than a comma but not as strong as a period. It should be used to separate elements that are <u>grammatically equal</u>.

1. Use a semicolon to separate clauses of a compound sentence that are not connected with a coordinating conjunction.

    <u>Pepper</u> <u>makes</u> me sneeze; <u>onions</u> <u>make</u> me cry.

    A semicolon by itself is as strong as a comma and *and* together.

$$; \quad = \quad , \quad + \quad \text{and}$$

<u>You should *not* use a semicolon to join unequal elements</u>, such as a dependent clause and an independent clause.

2. If commas are used within items in a series or within clauses in a compound sentence, use a semicolon instead of a comma to separate the items or clauses.

On our vacation we visited Springfield, Missouri; Springfield, Illinois; Springfield, Ohio; and Springfield, Massachusetts.

I enjoy woodworking, stamp collecting, and swimming; but my sister likes singing, dancing, and acting.

COLON

1. Use a colon to separate the hours from minutes in writing time.

2:35 p.m.

2. Use a colon after the salutation in a business letter.

Dear Ms. Schwartz:

3. Use a colon to introduce a list which follows an independent clause.

These are the things I need for school: paper, pencils, and pens.

Do not use a colon between the verb and its direct object.

INCORRECT: *For school I need: paper, pencils, and pens.*

CORRECT: *For school I need paper, pencils, and pens.*

APOSTROPHE

,

The apostrophe works a little differently from other punctuation marks. Instead of separating words, the apostrophe is actually part of a word. Using an apostrophe correctly is more a matter of spelling than of punctuation.

1. Use an apostrophe to replace omitted letters in a contraction.

    doesn't (does n**o**t)   you've (you **ha**ve)
    hasn't (has n**o**t)   o'clock (**of the** clock)

2. Use an apostrophe to show possession. To determine where to place the apostrophe, follow these steps.
    a. Ask yourself (in these words) TO WHOM DOES [ITEM] BELONG?
    b. Notice whether the answer to your question ends in *s*.
    c. If not, add *'s*; if so, add only an apostrophe.

    Example 1: *the man's hat*
    a. TO WHOM DOES THE HAT BELONG? *man*
    b. *Man* does not end in *s*.
    c. *'s* is added: *man's*

    Example 2: *the ladies' hats*
    a. TO WHOM DO THE HATS BELONG? *ladies*
    b. *Ladies* does end in *s*.
    c. Only an apostrophe is added: *ladies'*

    Example 3: *the children's toys*
    a. TO WHOM DO THE TOYS BELONG? *children*
    b. *Children* does not end in *s*.
    c. *'s* is added: *children's*

    Example 4: *Xerxes' army*
    a. TO WHOM DOES THE ARMY BELONG? *Xerxes* (zėrk´ zēz)
    b. *Xerxes* does end in *s*.
    c. Only an apostrophe is added: *Xerxes'*

79

For nouns and names ending in *s*, an *s* may be added after the apostrophe if you prefer a second *s* sound in the word:

boss**'s** policy   Marx**'s** theory
duchess**'s** wig   Jones**'s** house

Note that these are possessives, not plurals.

3. Use an apostrophe to write the plural of a letter or a symbol.

*Mississippi has four **i'**s and four **s'**s.*

Notice that the apostrophe is not used in forming other plurals.

HYPHEN

1. Use a hyphen in some compound words, in two-word numbers from twenty-one to ninety-nine, and in fractions used as adjectives.

jack-of-all-trades   a two-thirds majority

2. If a word will not fit on a line, use a hyphen to divide the word at the end of a syllable. Note that the hyphen goes after the first part of the word at the end of the line; the following line does not start with a hyphen. One-syllable words cannot be divided.

QUOTATION MARKS

Quotation marks always occur in pairs.

1. Use quotation marks to enclose exact words spoken.

"Where are you going?" Mom asked.

Mom asked, "Where are you going?"

The tag, indicating the speaker, is set off from the quotation with a comma unless a question mark or exclamation point is used. <u>A comma should never be used right next to a question mark or exclamation point</u>.

Notice that the first word of a direct quotation begins with a capital letter. If a tag is placed in the middle of a sentence, however, the first letter following the tag is lower-cased.

"Where," Mom asked, "are you going?"

If a tag is placed between sentences within a quotation, end punctuation is used either before or after the tag. The new sentence starts with a capital letter.

"Where are you going?" Mom asked. "You need to clean your room."

"Where are you going?" Mom reminded, "You need to clean your room."

If a direct quotation is longer than one sentence, place opening quotation marks at the beginning, and closing quotation marks at the end. Do not enclose each sentence individually.

"Where are you going? You need to clean your room," *Mom reminded.*

When writing a conversation involving two or more people, <u>start a new paragraph whenever you change speakers</u>.

Mom asked, "Where are you going, Mark?"
"Over to Raul's house to play," Mark replied.
"You must be forgetting that you need to clean your room before our company arrives," Mom reminded.
"Aw, gee," Mark grumbled, starting upstairs.

Do not use quotation marks if you are reporting what someone said without using exact words. This is called an **indirect quotation**. The word *that* often signals an indirect quotation.

*Mom reminded me **that** I needed to clean my room.*

If a quotation continues over several paragraphs (such as a story within a story), begin each new paragraph with opening quotation marks even though you have not used closing quotation marks. This reminds the reader that the material is quoted.

2. Use quotation marks to enclose titles of poems, stories, songs, and articles. In general, quotation marks are used for the titles of short pieces which would be part of a longer work. <u>Notice that these titles are not set off with commas</u>.

*Our Great Books group discussed **"The Nightingale."***

3. Use single quotation marks for a quotation or a title within a quotation.

*"Have you memorized **'Paul Revere's Ride'**?" Erica asked.*

*"Sam said, **'I refuse to go!'**" Kim reported to Dani.*

As you study the examples above, notice that <u>commas and periods are always placed inside closing quotation marks</u>. Question marks and exclamation points are placed inside if they are part of the quotation or title. Otherwise they are placed outside.

UNDERLINING (ITALICS)

1. Underline (or italicize) the title of a book, newspaper, magazine, play, or movie. In general, underlining is used for titles of longer works or for collections of shorter works. Titles of sacred

writings and government documents require neither quotation marks nor underlining.

> **_Star Wars_** *is an action-packed film with remarkable special effects.*

> *Did you read "The President's Toughest Decision" in a recent issue of* **_Parade_**?

> *Many people memorize passages from the* **Constitution** *and from the* **Bible**.

2. Underline the name of a specific ship, train, spaceship, etc.

> *The* **_Titanic_** *was supposed to be unsinkable.*

> *The explosion of the* **_Challenger_** *was a tragedy.*

3. Underline a word or phrase requiring special emphasis. The less often you use this, the more effective it will be. If you try to emphasize too much, you'll end up emphasizing nothing; everything will look the same. Too much underlining also tends to make writing look juvenile. Instead, you can emphasize by word choice or by other means of punctuation.

> INEFFECTIVE: *I was* **_not_** *offended by what* **_you_** *said.*

> EFFECTIVE: *I was not offended by what you said.*
> (This emphasis suggests that someone else might have been offended.)

4. Underline a word, letter, or other symbol if you are referring to the word or symbol itself rather than to the *meaning* it generally represents. This is something you may not use often; however, you have seen many examples of it in this book.

> *In formal writing you should spell out* **_and_** *rather than use* **_&_** *(called an ampersand). (In this sentence and means "the word* and;*" it does not carry* and*'s usual meaning or perform its usual function.)*

PARENTHESES ( )

Parentheses may be used to enclose information that could be omitted without changing the basic meaning of the sentence. Commas are sometimes used to enclose extra information as well. If you are trying to decide whether to use parentheses or a pair of commas, keep in mind that commas are less interruptive than parentheses. If the extra information is closely related to the sentence and commas make the meaning clear, you should use commas. If the extra information is more removed from the sentence or if meaning is unclear with commas (perhaps because you have other commas in the sentence), you should use parentheses.

Like quotation marks, parentheses are always used in pairs (one side of a pair of parentheses is called a **parenthesis**). When using parentheses within a sentence, begin the enclosed material with a lowercase letter.

*We were tired after our long drive (**twelve hours**).*

If the enclosed material is a question or exclamation, punctuate it accordingly (within the parentheses). Do not use a period inside the parentheses, however.

*We spent two hours (**every minute worthwhile!**) waiting in line to ride the Tower of Terror.*

If the parenthetical expression is inserted where a punctuation mark is needed in the sentence, the punctuation mark comes after—not before—the parenthetical expression.

*Because it rained (**two inches!**), the race was postponed.*

When using parentheses, be sure the sentence would be complete and logical if the parenthetical expression were omitted.

84

ILLOGICAL:	*You are an even better (**more versatile player**) than I realized.*
LOGICAL:	*You are an even better (**more versatile**) player than I realized.*

The frequent use of parentheses is distracting to the reader and shows an immature writing style. Whenever possible, make the parenthetical information part of the main sentence or omit it entirely.

We were tired after our twelve-hour drive.

DASH

1. A dash is used to indicate an interruption or a sudden shift in thought.

   "There seems to be something wrong with the ph—"
   Aaron said as the line went dead.

2. A pair of dashes may be used as a pair of parentheses—for non-essential information. Generally dashes are considered to be even more interruptive than commas or parentheses. They usually indicate a sudden shift in thought or provide greater emphasis than do commas or parentheses.

   *For whatever reason—**was it courage or foolishness?**—300 Greeks fought against 250,000 Persians at Thermopylae.*

If you use more than one dash within a sentence, be sure the dashes are a pair, enclosing one idea then taking your reader back to the main idea. A series of dashes might lead your reader farther and farther from your main idea.

Like parentheses, dashes should not be overused.

ELLIPSIS   •   •   •

An ellipsis indicates that you are omitting one or more words from material you are quoting. You might do that so your quotation will better focus on the point you are making.

> ORIGINAL: TV, though sometimes informative, can reduce a person's ability to think.

> AS QUOTED: "TV . . . can reduce a person's ability to think."

Notice that an ellipsis consists of three periods with space between them. If you were typing an ellipsis, you would hit the space bar once after each period.

The part of the quotation you are omitting might be at the beginning, in the middle, or at the end. If it is at the end of a sentence, you would have a fourth period, representing the period at the end of the sentence. <u>That is the only situation in which you would use more than three periods</u>.

Beware of ellipses (/i lip´ sēz/, the plural of ellipsis) used in advertising. The omission of certain words might have significantly changed the meaning of the quotation.

BRACKETS   [   ]

Brackets, which occur in pairs, may be used when you need to clarify the meaning of a quotation by adding words that were not in the original. Your version should in no way change the meaning or intent of the original material.

> *"The third President of the United States made a shrewd purchase **[the Louisiana Territory]** that doubled the size of the country."*

You might also put some words in brackets so that your quotation will blend more smoothly with the text before it.

*"[**Thomas Jefferson**] made a shrewd purchase that doubled the size of [**the United States**]."*

Although the previous example shows how to use brackets, the sentence would probably be better if it were reworded so that the quotation marks, and therefore the brackets, would be unnecessary.

SPELLING

Knowing a few spelling rules about adding prefixes and suffixes will help you to spell thousands of words correctly.

1 + 1 + 1 RULE

If a one-syllable word ends with a single consonant preceded by one short vowel, double the consonant before adding a suffix <u>beginning with a vowel</u>.

s t **o p** + **p** + (suffix) = sto**pp**ed, sto**pp**ing, sto**pp**er

Notice that the final consonant is *not* doubled if a root word ends in two consonants or in one consonant preceded by two vowels.

h e **l p** + (suffix) = he**lp**ed, he**lp**ing, he**lp**er

c l e **a** n + (suffix) = clea**n**ed, clea**n**ing, cleaner

1 + 1 + 1 APPLICATION FOR TWO-SYLLABLE WORDS

When adding a vowel suffix to a two-syllable word ending in a single consonant preceded by a single vowel, double the consonant <u>if the second syllable is accented</u>.

b e g **i n** + **n** + (suffix) = begin´**n**ing

$$\text{o c c } \textbf{u r} + \textbf{r} + \text{(suffix)} = \text{occur'red, occur'ring,}$$
$$\text{occur'rence}$$

$$\text{r e f } \textbf{e r} + \textbf{(r)} + \text{(suffix)} = \text{refer'red, refer'ring,}$$
$$\text{ref'erence}$$

Notice in the last example above that the *r* is not doubled when the accent is on the first syllable.

WORDS ENDING IN SILENT *E*

When a word ends with a silent *e*, drop the *e* before adding a suffix <u>beginning with a vowel</u>.

h o p **e** + (suffix) = hoped, hoping

Notice that the silent *e* is usually kept before a suffix <u>beginning with a consonant</u>.

hop**eful**　　care**less**　　lon**ely**　　mov**ement**　　fals**ehood**

The following words are common EXCEPTIONS to the preceding rule. The silent *e* in the root word has been dropped even though the suffix begins with a consonant.

argument　　　truly　　　wholly

A silent *e* is not dropped before a suffix beginning with *a* or *o* if that *e* is needed to keep a *c* or *g* from becoming hard.

mana**ge** + able = mana**ge**able

noti**ce** + able = noti**ce**able

WORDS ENDING IN *Y*

Words ending in *y* preceded by a consonant generally change *y* to *i* before all suffixes *except* those beginning with an *i*.

$$\overset{i}{\text{tr} \cancel{y}} \quad + \text{ (suffix)} = \text{tr}\textbf{ies}, \text{tr}\textbf{ied}$$

$$\overset{i}{\text{eas} \cancel{y}} \quad + \text{ (suffix)} = \text{eas}\textbf{ier}, \text{eas}\textbf{iest}, \text{eas}\textbf{ily}$$

$$\overset{i}{\text{happ} \cancel{y}} \quad + \text{ (suffix)} = \text{happ}\textbf{ier}, \text{happ}\textbf{iest}, \text{happ}\textbf{iness}$$

$$\overset{i}{\text{beaut} \cancel{y}} \quad + \text{ (suffix)} = \text{beaut}\textbf{iful}, \text{beaut}\textbf{ify}$$

Note these examples where the *y* is not dropped before a suffix beginning with *i*.

trying   **carrying**   **studying**   **babyish**   **lobbyist**

In words where *y* is preceded by a vowel, the *y* is not dropped, whether the suffix begins with a vowel or with a consonant.

keys   **played**   **obeying**   **joyful**   **employment**

A common EXCEPTION to the preceding rule is the irregularly spelled word *paid*.

PLURALS

The plural of a noun is the form of the word that indicates more than one. Unless a noun forms its plural by following one of the first two rules discussed below, you could find the plural form in the dictionary entry for that noun. It usually appears in boldface type near the beginning of the entry and is identified as a plural with *pl*.

1. Most nouns form their plural simply by adding *s*.

day	day**s**		elephant	elephant**s**
smile	smile**s**		chimney	chimney**s**

2. Nouns that end in *s*, *sh*, *ch*, *x*, or *z* form their plural by adding *es*. The extra syllable that results is necessary to make the words pronounceable.

dress	dress**es**		chur**ch**	chur**ches**
bru**sh**	bru**shes**		bo**x**	bo**xes**
			waltz	waltz**es**

3. Nouns that end in *y* preceded by a consonant form their plural by changing *y* to *i* and adding *-es*.

ci**ti**~~y~~	cit**ies**		countr**i**~~y~~	countr**ies**
la**di**~~y~~	lad**ies**		famil**i**~~y~~	famil**ies**

4. Most nouns that end in *f* or *fe* form their plural by adding *s*. Some such nouns form their plural by changing *f* or *fe* to *ves*. In most cases, a *v* in the plural can be heard when the word is pronounced correctly.

gulf	gulf**s**		chief	chief**s**
belie**f**	belie**fs**		loaf	loa**ves**
half	hal**ves**		thief	thie**ves**
wol**f**	wol**ves**		life	li**ves**
kni**fe**	kni**ves**		self	sel**ves**
wi**fe**	wi**ves**		leaf	lea**ves**

5. Nouns that end in *o* preceded by a vowel usually form their plural by adding *s*.

rad**io**	radios		pat**io**	patios
z**oo**	zoos		rod**eo**	rodeos

Nouns ending in *o* preceded by a consonant generally form their plural by adding *-es*.

he**ro**	hero**es**		toma**to**	tomato**es**
ve**to**	veto**es**		mosqui**to**	mosquito**es**

Many EXCEPTIONS to the preceding rule are words that have to do with music. They form their plural simply by adding *s*.

al**to**	altos		pia**no**	pianos
so**lo**	solos		soprano	sopranos

Some nouns ending in *o* preceded by a consonant have two correct spellings for their plural forms. Whenever a dictionary shows alternatives, the preferred form is given first.

zero	zeros *or* zeroes	torna**do**	tornados *or* tornadoes
ho**bo**	hobos *or* hoboes	volcano	volcanos *or* volcanoes

6. Some nouns form their plural irregularly.

man	men	louse	lice
woman	women	foot	feet
child	children	tooth	teeth
mouse	mice	goose	geese

7. Some nouns do not change their spelling from singular to plural.

deer   sheep   trout   moose   salmon

A few nouns have two correct spellings for their plural forms, one which is identical to the singular form and another which is formed in the regular way.

fish *or* fishes	shrimp *or* shrimps
pair *or* pairs	youth *or* youths

8. Some nouns that have come to English from other languages
   form their plurals irregularly. Some have two correct forms.

alumnus	alumni	larva	larvae
analysis	analyses	phenomenon	phenomena
crisis	crises	phylum	phyla
datum	data	radius	radii *or* radiuses
formula	formulas *or* formulae	stadium	stadiums *or* stadia
		stimulus	stimuli

ADDING PREFIXES

Generally a prefix is added without changing the spelling of the root
word. Therefore, it is helpful to know the spellings of both prefixes
and roots. Notice that if a root begins with the same letter a prefix
ends with, the new word will have a double letter.

un	+ necessary	=	**unn**ecessary
over	+ rule	=	ove**rr**ule
il	+ legal	=	i**ll**egal
dis	+ appear	=	di**s**appear
dis	+ satisfy	=	di**ss**atisfy

WORDS EASILY CONFUSED

When words have similar spellings, people need to find ways to
remember which spelling to use in each situation. Sentences or
illustrations, such as those used here, might help you to remember
correct spellings. Try creating some of your own!

1. accept—except

Accept means "to receive."

*Please **accept** this package.*

Except means "leaving out; but."

*All exits **except** one were blocked.*

2. advice—advise

Advice (ad vīs´) is a noun.

*She was nice and gave me good **advice**.*

Advise (ad vīz´) is a verb.

*I will ask the wise person to **advise** me.*

3. affect—effect

Affect is a verb meaning "to act on; to change."

*How do holidays **affect** the mood of the staff?*

Effect is usually a noun meaning "result."

*What is the **effect** of sunlight on plant growth?*

Effect is occasionally used as a verb meaning "to make happen; to bring about."

*Because the cancer was discovered early, doctors were able to **effect** a cure.*

4. angel—angle

Angel means "a heavenly being." (Notice that *g* followed by *e* is soft.)

*Angela portrayed an **angel** in the pageant.*

Angle means "the shape made when two straight lines meet." (Notice that *g* followed by a consonant is hard.)

*The triangle had three 60-degree **angles**.*

5. are—our

Many people pronounce these words the same. However, more precise pronunciation may help you to use the words correctly.

Are (är) is a form of the verb *to be.*

*You **are** my best friend.*

Our (our—*ou* as in *out*) is a possessive pronoun.

***Our** house is on the corner.*

6. desert—dessert

Desert (dez´ ėrt), as a noun, means "an area getting little rain."

*Camels used to be known as the "ships of the **desert**."*

Desert (də zėrt´), as a verb, means "to leave; to abandon."

*The frightened soldier was tempted to **desert** the army.*

Dessert (də zėrt´) means "the final course of a meal." You might remember that *dessert* has an extra *s* because dessert is something extra at a meal.

*We had peach cobbler for **dessert**.*

7. every day—everyday

Every day is two words meaning "each day."

> **Every day** *I get up at 7:00.*

Everyday is an adjective meaning "ordinary; not special."

> *Meeting a famous person is not an* **everyday** *event.*

8. have—of—off

Have is a verb, often a helping verb.

> *You should* **have** *recycled those aluminum cans.*

Of (uv) is a preposition.

> *My little brother got a new box* **of** *crayons.*

Off (of) is a preposition. It should not be used with *of*.

> *I brushed the fly* **off** *my arm.*

9. it's—its

It's is a contraction for *it is*.

> **It's** *a beautiful day.*

Its is a possessive pronoun.

> *The chair is uneven because* **its** *leg is broken.*

10. know—now

Know (nō)

> *Do you* **know** *the answer?*

Now rhymes with *cow*.

The <u>cow</u> is **<u>now</u>** in the pasture.

11. loose—lose

Loose (lüs) means "not tight."

Her t<u>oo</u>th is **l<u>oo</u>se**.

Lose (lüz) means "to mislay" or "to suffer loss."

Be careful not to **l<u>o</u>se** the <u>ro</u>se.

We don't want to **lose** the game.

12. passed—past

Passed is the past tense form of the regular verb *pass*.

She **passed** the salt.

The dieter quickly **passed** the bakery.

As a noun *past* refers to time that has gone by.

Historians study the **past**.

Past can also be a preposition.

He walked <u>fast</u> **<u>past</u>** the <u>last</u> bakery.

13. quit—quite—quiet

Paying careful attention to the pronunciation indicated by the spelling pattern in these words will help you to use them correctly.

Quit (kwit), which follows the typical short vowel pattern, means "to stop."

> **Quit** *bothering me!*

Quite (kwīt), which follows the typical vowel-consonant-*e* pattern, means "to a great extent."

> *I felt* **quite** *satisfied with my essay.*

Quiet (kwī´et) means "not loud." Notice that the two vowels are in different syllables.

> *It is important to be* **quiet** *in a hospital.*

14. than—then

Than is used in comparisons.

> *D<u>an</u> has a better pl<u>an</u>* **th<u>an</u>** *St<u>an</u>.*

Then is used to indicate time.

> *K<u>en</u> put the h<u>en</u> in the p<u>en</u>;* **th<u>en</u>** *he w<u>en</u>t to the d<u>en</u>.*

15. there—their—they're

There indicates place. (Notice that other place words end in *ere*: *here*, *where*.)

> *She was already* **there** *when I arrived.*

There is sometimes used to start sentences in which the subject follows the verb.

> **There** *<u>are</u> three <u>ways</u> to wear this hat.*

Their is a possessive pronoun.

> *That house has been in* **their** *family for eighty years.*

They're is a contraction for *they are*.

They're *planning to go ice skating this afternoon.*

16. **to—too—two**

To is a preposition.

He gave the book ***to*** *me.*

To is often used with the infinitive form of the verb.

He wants ***to*** *become an architect.*

Too means "also" or "more than enough." (You might remember this by thinking of the word as having "more than enough" *o*'s.)

I want to go, ***too***.

The box was ***too*** *large for one person to carry.*

Two is a number.

I have ***two*** *sisters.*

17. **wear—where—were**

Pronouncing these words correctly will help you to use them correctly.

Wear (wâr) means "to carry on the body."

It's a great day to <u>w**ear**</u> *my new* <u>earmuffs</u>.

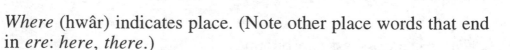

Where (hwâr) indicates place. (Note other place words that end in *ere*: *here*, *there*.)

Where *are my tennis shoes?*

Were (wėr) is a past form of the verb *to be*.

*We **were** working in the garden when she arrived.*

18. weather—whether

Weather (weᴛʜ´ ėr) means "outside conditions, such as temperature, precipitation, and sunshine."

*I hope the **weather** will be nice for our picnic.*

Whether (hweᴛʜ´ ėr) is a subordinating conjunction expressing doubt. When the word is pronounced correctly, you will hear a blast of air before the *w* sound. If you put your hand in front of your mouth, you should be able to feel this air, which you should not feel when you pronounce *weather*.

*I have to ask my parents **whether** I can go to the mall.*

19. which—witch

The difference in pronunciation between these two words is the same as that between *whether* and *weather* discussed above.

Which (hwich) may introduce a dependent clause.

*The book **which** I returned to the library was overdue.*

Which may indicate a choice.

***Which** do you prefer?*

Witch (wich) means "a person believed to have magical powers."

*I s<u>titch</u>ed my <u>itchy</u> **witch** costume for Halloween.*

20. who's—whose

Who's is a contraction for *who is*.

***Who's** ready to dive into the pool?*

Whose is the possessive form of *who*.

Whose *jacket is this?*

21. **you're—your**

You're is a contraction for *you are*.

You're *asking for trouble.*

Your is a possessive pronoun.

What is **your** *favorite hobby?*

WORDS COMMONLY MISSPELLED

Check this list often so that you will spell these words correctly. Add other words that are troublesome for you.

a lot	eighth	minute	soccer
again	embarrass		speech
allowed	equipment	necessary	stopped
always	every	ninety	straight
answer			studying
Arctic	February	once	supposed
argument	finally		sure
	foreign	paid	surprise
before	fortunately	perform	
beginning	forty	probably	they
bicycle	friend		through
built		ready	tired
business	government	really	tomorrow
	guess	receive	trouble
coming		recommend	
completely	happened		until
	height	safety	upon
definite		said	
describe	interesting	science	Wednesday
disappear		second	which
disappoint	judgment	sentence	woman (sing.)
doesn't		separate	women (pl.)
	knowledge	since	

100

COMMUNICATING IDEAS

Spend a few moments trying to think without using words.

Were you able to do that? Probably not. The words and structure of our language determine, to some extent, how we think.

In addition to helping us think, language enables us to share ideas. Have you ever tried to communicate with someone who did not speak or understand your language? A few ideas, such as heat, cold, or hunger, can be communicated with gestures. However, communication between people who do not share a language is very limited.

On the other hand, *with* the tool of language, the possibilities for communication are almost endless. The author Homer of ancient Greece so precisely described the geographical features around the city of Troy that German archaeologist Heinrich Schliemann was able to locate the site nearly 3,000 years later! Many writers are able to arrange the squiggles of ink that we call letters in such a way that they move us to terror, agony, joy, or other emotions.

In this section you will find ways to strengthen your ability to manipulate ideas, whether you are receiving those ideas through reading or are sharing your original ideas through writing. As you improve your language ability, you will also improve your thinking skills.

VOCABULARY

As mentioned in the introduction to this book, English has acquired words from around the world. Becoming familiar with many words will help you to understand what you read. You will also have a wide selection of words when you're writing.

Looking up every unfamiliar word you encounter could become an arduous task—and not necessarily worthwhile. Learning how to determine a word's meaning from the way the word is used in a sentence is a much more practical and valuable skill.

If, however, you would add just one new word each day to your vocabulary (in addition, of course, to the words your teachers ask you to learn), in a year you would have learned 365 new words! Make your family aware of *any* words that you are learning, in school or on your own. The more you see and hear those words in sentences, the better you will understand them. You should make an effort to *use* new words, too—in your speech and in your writing.

MORPHEMES

A **morpheme** is the smallest unit of meaning in a word. In many cases a whole word is a single morpheme.

> look　　giraffe　　picture　　view

Often, however, a word consists of a root or base word with prefixes and/or suffixes attached. If you know the meaning of each of these parts, you can "add them up" and figure out the meaning of the word. For example, the -*s* morpheme at the end of a noun indicates a plural. The -*ed* morpheme at the end of a verb indicates past tense; *re-* at the beginning of a word means "back" or "again."

> giraffe + s = giraffes　　re + view + ed = reviewed

Notice that the letters themselves are not *always* morphemes and do not always have these meanings. *Re* in *picture* or *read*, for example, is not a morpheme. It is not a separate unit of meaning; the two letters are simply part of a longer morpheme.

Many English morphemes originated in other languages. *Hippopotamus*, for example, combines the Greek morpheme *hippos*, meaning "horse," with the Greek morpheme *potamos*, meaning "river." The hippopotamus is, literally, a "river horse."

Knowing the meanings of common morphemes can help you figure out the meanings of thousands of words the first time you see them. In the list below, a morpheme followed by a hyphen would be used at the beginning of a word as a prefix; a morpheme preceded by a hyphen would be used at the end of a word as a suffix. Since a suffix determines a word's part of speech, the part of speech is shown with each suffix's meaning. A morpheme in the list without a hyphen is a root and could have prefixes or suffixes attached to it. In some cases a morpheme has more than one spelling or the spelling might change slightly as the morpheme attaches to the rest of a word.

Morpheme and Meaning	Examples
a-, an- (not; without)	atheist, amoral, apathy, anarchy
ab- (away; from)	abnormal, abject, abrupt, abstract
-able (capable of) (adj.)	changeable, dependable, reliable
-acy (quality or state of) (n.)	privacy, delicacy, lunacy, conspiracy
ad- (to, toward)	administer, adhere, advent, admit
-al (having to do with) (adj.)	national, regional, emotional
ambi-, amphi- (both)	amphibian, ambiguity, ambivalent
anim (life; mind; soul)	animal, animation, unanimous
ann (year)	annual, anniversary, annuity
ante- (before)	antecedent, anteroom, antebellum
anthropo (mankind)	anthropomorphic, philanthropist
anti- (against)	antisocial, antidote, antifreeze
arch- (chief; principal)	archenemy, monarch, archbishop
aster, astr (star)	astronaut, asterisk, disaster, aster
-ate (cause to be) (v.)	educate, duplicate, manipulate
-ative (tending toward) (adj.)	talkative, negative, decorative

103

Morpheme and Meaning	Examples

aud (hear) 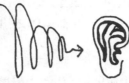   auditory, audience, audit, audition

auto (self)   automobile, autobiography, autocrat

bene (good, well)   benefit, benediction, benevolent

bi- (two)   bicycle, bisect, bilateral, bicameral

biblio (book)   bibliography, Bible, bibliophile

bio (life)   biology, biography, biodegradable

cap (head)   capital, captain, per capita, capitulate

cent (hundred)   century, percent, centennial

cent (center)   central, concentric, egocentric

chrom (color)   monochromatic, chromosome

chron (time)   chronology, chronic, anachronism

cide (kill)   homicide, suicide, insecticide

circum (around) 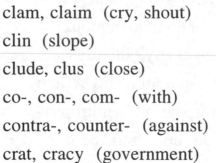 circumference, circuit, circus

clam, claim (cry, shout)   exclaim, proclaim, clamor, declaim

clin (slope)   incline, recline, inclination, decline

clude, clus (close)   include, conclusion, preclude

co-, con-, com- (with)   cooperate, concur, companion

contra-, counter- (against)   contrast, counterattack, contradict

crat, cracy (government)   democracy, autocracy, aristocrat

cred (believe)   credibility, credit, incredible, creed

cycle (circle)   bicycle, cyclone, encyclopedia

de- (down; from)   depose, detract, describe, deduct

dec, deci (ten)   decimal, decade, decathlon, decibel

Morpheme and Meaning	Examples
dem (people)	democracy, epidemic, demography
derm (skin)	dermis, dermatologist, hypodermic
dia- (across; through)	diameter, dialogue, diagram, dialysis
dict (say) 	dictate, predict, verdict, diction
dis- (not; opposite)	dislike, disappear, disappoint
duc (lead)	induce, conduct, duke, educate
en-, em- (make; give)	enable, encourage, empower
-en (make; give) (v.)	sweeten, harden, strengthen
epi- (on, over)	epilogue, epitaph, epidermis
-er (more) (adj.)	louder, softer, prettier, handier
-er (one who) (n.)	baker, washer, crier, pitcher
eu- (good, well)	euphemism, euthanasia, eulogy
ex- (out)	exhale, exit, exterior, exception
ex- (former)	ex-spouse, ex-president, ex-convict
extra- (outside)	extracurricular, extraordinary
fac, fic (make; do)	factory, fiction, artifact, manufacture
fin (end; limit)	final, infinite, definition, definite
flect, flex (bend) 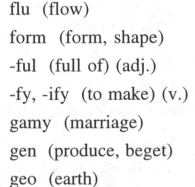	reflect, deflect, inflection, flexible
flu (flow)	fluid, fluent, fluctuate, confluence
form (form, shape)	inform, reform, conform, deform
-ful (full of) (adj.)	colorful, thankful, wonderful
-fy, -ify (to make) (v.)	simplify, magnify, beautify, deify
gamy (marriage)	monogamy, bigamy, polygamy
gen (produce, beget)	generation, generous, genealogy
geo (earth)	geography, geology, geophysics

Morpheme and Meaning	Examples
gnos (knowledge)	agnostic, ignorant, diagnosis
grad, gress (step)	gradual, graduation, progress
graph, gram (write)	photograph, phonograph, telegram
-hood (state of) (n.)	childhood, statehood, likelihood
hyper (above; excessive)	hyperactive, hypercritical, hyperbole
hypo (under; insufficient)	hypodermic, hypothesis, hypocrisy
-ible (capable of) (adj.)	divisible, legible, horrible, edible
-ic (having to do with) (adj.)	democratic, chronic, civic, enigmatic
in-, im- (in, into)	inside, include, income, import
in-, im-, il-, ir- (not)	inactive, impure, illegal, irregular
inter- (between, among)	intermission, interrupt, interject
intra-, intro- (within)	intramural, introvert, intravenous
-ish (like; somewhat) (adj.)	childish, selfish, reddish, sluggish
-ism (doctrine of) (n.)	conservatism, patriotism, criticism
-ist (one who) (n.)	artist, loyalist, dramatist, realist
-itis (inflammation of) (n.)	tonsillitis, appendicitis, sinusitis
-ity (state of) (n.)	acidity, locality, familiarity, humidity
-ive (tending toward) (adj.)	active, destructive, sensitive, native
-ize (to make) (v.)	memorize, modernize, customize

ject (throw)	inject, reject, dejected, subject
junc (join)	junction, conjunction, injunction
-less (without) (adj.)	hopeless, careless, countless
log, logy (study of)	catalog, biology, psychology
log, loc, loq (speak)	monologue, elocution, colloquial

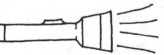

lumin, luc (light)　illuminate, lucid, Lucifer

Morpheme and Meaning	Examples
-ly (in the manner of) (adv.)	slowly, freely, happily, angrily
mal- (bad)	malnutrition, malignant, malice
man (hand)	manual, manicure, manuscript
-ment (act or condition of) (n.)	government, refreshment, ornament
merg, mers (dip)	emerge, submerge, immersion
meter, metro (measure)	metric, thermometer, geometry

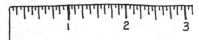

mis- (wrong; ill)	mislead, misunderstand, misread
mit, miss (send)	transmit, permission, missile
mon, mono (one)	monotone, monologue, monorail
-mony (resulting condition) (n.)	harmony, testimony, matrimony
mov, mot (move)	movie, motion, promote, mobile
multi- (many)	multiply, multitude, multicolored
-ness (condition) (n.)	kindness, happiness, rudeness
non- (not)	nonstop, nonconformist, nonfiction
-oid (in the form of) (adj., n.)	asteroid, mongoloid, trapezoid
omni- (all)	omnipotent, omniscient, omnivore
-or (one who or which) (n.)	governor, conqueror, motor
-ose, -ous (full of) (adj.)	famous, porous, verbose, comatose
-osis (state of) (n.)	hypnosis, tuberculosis, osteoporosis
pan- (all; universal)	panacea, panorama, Pan-American
para- (beside)	parallel, paraphrase, parasite
path (feeling)	sympathy, apathetic, pathology
ped, pod (foot)	pedal, tripod, pedestrian, impede
pel, puls (push; drive)	expel, impulse, propel, dispel
pend, pens (hang; weigh)	pendulum, suspenders, suspense

Morpheme and Meaning	Examples
penta- (five)	pentagon, Pentateuch, pentathlon
per- (through)	perforate, perceive, perfume
peri- (around)	perimeter, peripheral, periscope
phil (love)	Philadelphia, philosophy, philatelist
phobia (fear)	claustrophobia, hydrophobia
phon (sound)	phonograph, telephone, symphony
photo (light)	photography, photosynthesis
plic (fold) 	duplicate, implicate, complicate
plor (cry out)	implore, explore, deplorable
pneuma (wind, air)	pneumonia, pneumatic. pneuma
poly- (much, many)	polygon, polyester, polygraph
port (carry)	porter, import, portable, teleport
pos (to place)	pose, deposit, impose, position
post- (after)	postpone, postwar, postscript
pre- (before)	precede, precaution, prefix
press (press)	express, depress, impression
pro- (forward)	proceed, prospect, progress
pseudo (false)	pseudonym, pseudointellectual
psych (mind)	psychology, psychiatry, psychic
quad- (four)	quadrilateral, quadruped, quadruple
quint- (five)	quintuplet, quintet, quintile
re- (back)	reverse, retrieve, return, refund
re- (again)	review, replay, recopy, rebuild
retro- (backward)	retrorocket, retroactive, retrograde
rupt (break)	disrupt, interrupt, eruption, abrupt

108

Morpheme and Meaning	Examples

scope (see)  telescope, microscope, stethoscope

scrib, script (write)   prescribe, inscription, scribble

semi- (half, partly)   semicircle, semicolon, semiannual

sent, sens (feel)   sense, sensitive, sentimental, resent

-ship (quality or state) (n.)   friendship, leadership, scholarship

sist (stand)   insist, assist, exist, consist, resist

soma (body)   psychosomatic, somatology

spec, spic (look, appear)   inspect, spectacle, conspicuous

spir (breathe)   inspire, aspire, perspiration, expire

struct (build)   construct, destruct, instruct

sub- (under)   submarine, submit, subscribe

sult (jump)   insult, exultant, assault, result

sume, sumpt (take)   assume, consume, presumptuous

super- (over)   superlative, supersonic, superior

sym, syn (together)   symphony, synonym, symbol

tact, tang (touch)   contact, tangible, tactile, tangent

tain, ten, tin (hold)   contain, tenant, pertinent, detain

tele (far)   telephone, television, telekinesis

tend, tens (stretch)   extend, tension, tendency, intense

tetra- (four)   tetrahedron, tetrad, tetrology

theo (God, god)   theology, atheism, monotheism

therm (heat)   thermometer, thermostat, thermos

tract (pull)   tractor, retractable, attract, traction

Morpheme and Meaning	Examples
trans- (across)	transcontinental, translate, transfer
tri- (three)	tricycle, triangle, trinity, trio
-tude (quality of) (n.)	solitude, attitude, multitude, latitude
ultra- (beyond)	ultramodern, ultrasound, ultraviolet
un- (not; opposite)	unhappy, unlucky, untie, unfasten
uni- (one)	unison, unicorn, unicycle, unique
ven (come)	adventure, intervene, circumvent
verg (to lean)	verge, converge, divergent
vert, vers (turn)	invert, reverse, converse, version
vis (see)	vision, invisible, supervisor
voc, voke (call)	vocation, vocal, invoke, revoke
volv (turn)	revolve, evolve, involve, revolution

Try combining the morphemes in different ways. Also try combining them with other morphemes. You will increase your vocabulary!

UNDERSTANDING A DICTIONARY ENTRY

Understanding all parts of a dictionary entry can make a wealth of information available to you. Notice the parts of the entry below.

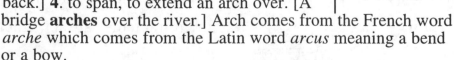

a   b   c   d   e   f   g   h

arch (ärch) *h.* pl. **arch´es 1.** a curved structure which is capable of supporting the weight of material over an open space. [Doorways, windows, bridges, etc. are often **arches**.] **2.** anything curved in the shape of an arch. [the **arch** of the foot] *v.* **arched, arch ing 3.** to cause to bend into an arch. [A cat can **arch** its back.] **4.** to span, to extend an arch over. [A bridge **arches** over the river.] Arch comes from the French word *arche* which comes from the Latin word *arcus* meaning a bend or a bow.

Reprinted by permission of Milliken Publishing Co.

110

a. The **entry word** appears in boldface type. It shows the spelling and syllable divisions of the word.

b. The **pronunciation** follows the entry word. Check the pronunciation key to learn the sounds indicated by the diacritical marks.

c. The **part of speech** is usually indicated by an abbreviation in italics. There may be more than one part of speech.

d. **Inflections**, such as plurals of nouns or principal parts of verbs, usually appear in boldface type.

e. **Definitions** are numbered. More common definitions appear earlier in the entry.

f. A **sentence** may illustrate the use of the word. This may appear in brackets or italics.

g. The **origin** of the word may be shown near the beginning or end.

h. A **picture** may help clarify the meaning of the word.

READING

Reading is a popular leisure activity as well as an important way of getting information. Knowing word meanings, sentence structure, and mechanics will help you understand what you read. Longer passages will be easier to read if you notice how they are organized and consider how they relate to what you already know. Become an active reader!

S Q 3 R

The SQ3R method, explained on the following pages, will help you to read efficiently. With this method, you will get the most from textbooks, articles, and other informative material in the shortest time.

1. **Surveying**. In surveying (or previewing) a chapter or an article, read the following:

> title
> introduction
> headings
> study aids (vocabulary, questions, graphic material, captions)
> conclusion

As you preview, begin relating what you will read to what you already know—from school and from your own experience. Think as you read. Notice how the chapter is organized. Prepare to fit details into this general organization.

2. **Questioning**. The material itself contains some questions, and  others have probably occurred to you during your previewing. Now turn each heading into a question that you might reasonably expect the section to answer. Make predictions about what will happen or what you will learn. Of course, you must be willing to revise your predictions as you get more information.

3. **Reading**. Read each section to find answers to your questions. This gives purpose to your reading. You are no longer simply reading words; you are reading to find important information. The information will be easier for you to understand and remember if you constantly relate new information to what you already know. Making mental pictures of what you are reading also makes the material more meaningful.

4. **Reciting**. When you finish reading each section, pause to see if  you have found the answers to your questions. If not, look through the section again. Sometimes you might find that the section did not provide the information you expected. Then you need to make a new important question and find its answer. Remember: If you can't understand material when you read it, there's no way you'll be able to remember it an hour later, or the next day, or at test time.

5. **Reviewing**. At the end of each article or chapter, review what you have read. You may do this by thinking through what you have learned, by glancing at headings, or by some other method. Ask yourself what the details of the chapter or article add up to. What main points are being made? Take time to think about how material you have read relates to what you already knew. You may want to jot down some brief notes to review when test time approaches. Look over your notes, or review material, often.

These steps may be adapted to meet your needs. Try to find the method that will work best for you.

USING SIGNAL WORDS

Noticing signal words will help you see how ideas are related.

1. *And*, *in addition*, and *furthermore* tell you that the next information will agree with previous information.

2. *But*, *however*, *although*, and *on the contrary* indicate that the next information will *contrast* with what you just read. You make a sharp turn in your reading.

3. *First*, *second*, and *third* signal a series of similar items. They might be reasons, or they might be steps in a procedure. Words like *next*, *then*, and *after* also indicate a sequence of steps or events.

4. *For example*, *specifically*, and *namely* show that the next idea will illustrate the idea that was just presented.

5. Noticing the use of **pronouns** or **synonyms** will also help you to see how ideas are related.

Understanding the relationship between ideas will help you find the ideas that are most important.

113

VISUALIZING

To visualize means "to make a picture in the mind." Before television was invented, many people used to listen to radio dramas, each person creating his or her own version of the action. Today movies, television, and even MTV provide pictures for us.

Whether you are enjoying a story or learning information, creating mental pictures when you listen or read will bring the words to life for you. Ideas will be easier to remember if you are visualizing and are not simply manipulating words.

As you visualize, feel free to add details that the text does not supply. For example, make a mental picture from the following sentence.

Sam bought peanuts from the vendor at the baseball game.

Do you picture Sam and the vendor as male or female? How old are they? Does the vendor work at a concession stand or walk up and down the aisles of a stadium? Is the game, in fact, a major league game or a little league game? What is the weather—sunny, hot, overcast, raining? Does the vendor seem to enjoy selling peanuts? How is this vendor different from other vendors?

As you add details, be careful that your picture does not contradict anything the text told you. For example, if, after reading the bold-face sentence, you pictured a basketball game, you would have ignored or changed information you had been given. Similarly, if you later get information that does not fit with your picture, you need to be willing to revise it. If, for example, you pictured a hot, sunny day and later learn that it is raining, you need to revisualize.

When you are reading, replay this "movie in your mind" frequently. Read and replay important sections carefully to be sure you have the correct picture. Then replay those sections so that you will remember the image. Consider how many times an amazing or controversial play in a sports contest might be replayed on television. Each time you see it, you fix it more firmly in your mind so that you could more vividly describe it. That's what you are doing as you replay pictures of what you are reading. You are fixing the material in your mind so that you will remember it.

OUTLINING

An outline helps you to see the relationship between ideas. It can be useful for taking notes from your reading, for taking notes in class, or for organizing a composition you plan to write.

The main ideas in an outline are indicated by Roman numerals. Points supporting main ideas are indented and are indicated by capital letters. Details supporting these subpoints are further indented and are indicated by Arabic numerals. Minor details, which support more important details, are indented still further and are indicated by lowercase letters. You can make a more detailed outline by using parentheses and brackets and by alternating numbers and letters. However, such a detailed outline is usually impractical.

Parallel points in an outline are subdivisions of the preceding more important point. Since nothing can be divided into only one part, you should never have only one subdivision. Thus, if a subpoint has a *1*, it should also have a *2*; if a detail has an *a*, it should also have a *b*.

Although your outlines will not be this long, knowing **Roman numerals** will help you recognize them in other situations.

I = 1	X = 10	C = 100	M = 1,000
V = 5	L = 50	D = 500	

No more than one V, L, or D is ever used together. No more than three I's, X's, or C's are ever used together. To show 4 or 9 (or 40, 90, 400, 900, etc.), an I, an X, or a C is shown to the left of a larger symbol to indicate an amount *less* than that of the larger symbol. Amounts greater than the symbol are shown to the right.

III = 3	IX = 9	XXXIV = 34	LX = 60
IV = 4	XI = 11	XXXIX = 39	XC = 90
VI = 6	XIX = 19	XL = 40	CD = 400
VIII = 8	XXX = 30	XLIX = 49	MCMXCIX = 1999

The sample outline on the next page shows outline form with proper subordination. It includes the same material as the discussion of the writing process on pages 117 through 120. Comparing the outline with the explanation may give you an idea how you can outline what you read or how you can use an outline to plan your writing.

THE WRITING PROCESS

I. Pre-writing
- A. Define your task
  - 1. Choose your topic
  - 2. Know your audience
  - 3. Know your purpose
- B. Plan
  - 1. Jot down your ideas
  - 2. Determine your order

II. Writing the first draft
- A. Get your ideas down quickly
- B. Don't worry about mechanics
- C. Write on only one side of the page
- D. Skip lines

III. Polishing
- A. Evaluate your own work
  - 1. Is your composition complete?
  - 2. Is your composition clear?
  - 3. Have you sufficiently supported your ideas?
  - 4. Have you created vivid pictures for the reader?
  - 5. Is everything geared toward your purpose?
  - 6. Will your lead gain the reader's attention?
  - 7. Will your conclusion leave the desired impression?
  - 8. Do sentences sound smooth?
- B. Conference—focus on content
  - 1. Read composition aloud to someone else
  - 2. Ask listener to "tell back" what was heard
  - 3. Ask which parts work well
  - 4. Ask for suggestions
  - 5. Ask open-ended questions
- C. Revise
  - 1. Consider all suggestions
  - 2. Make improvements
- D. Edit—Check one thing at a time
  - 1. Complete sentences
  - 2. Paragraphing
  - 3. Usage
  - 4. Capitalization
  - 5. Punctuation
  - 6. Spelling

IV. Making your final copy
- A. Allow margins
- B. Make copy neat
- C. Proofread by repeating editing steps (III-D above)

116

WRITING

Writing is a very complex process because your brain must tend to many different things at once: you must form your idea, put it into words, think about how to spell those words, consider what to capitalize and how to punctuate, *and* remember how to form letters. In addition, while you are writing one sentence, your mind is likely racing ahead to what you will say in the *next* sentence!

Although detailed instruction in writing is beyond the scope of this book, a few suggestions are offered along with models that might answer some of your questions about particular kinds of writing.

THE WRITING PROCESS

One way to make writing easier is to break the process into parts so that you can focus on each step individually. At any time, even when you are trying to decide what you will write about, you might find it helpful to talk about your ideas with someone else.

1. Clarify your writing task. Be sure you know whom you are writing for and why. Don't think of your **audience** merely as your teacher. Hopefully your writing will be read by others—classmates, perhaps, or readers of a school newspaper. Even if your teacher is the main person who will see your work, however, imagine that you are writing for a specific, perhaps broader, audience—your peers, younger students, a famous author, a relative. Also have the **purpose** of your writing clearly in mind. What do you want your writing to accomplish? What response do you want from your readers?

2. Once you have determined your audience and purpose, spend some time jotting down ideas and **planning** your writing—whether it be a story, a poem, a report, an essay, or something else. How will you accomplish your purpose? Your ideas might be in the form of an outline or a web, or they might just be scattered randomly on a page. The important thing is to record them somewhere so you don't have to worry about forgetting them. That frees your mind for writing.

3. Once you have gathered your ideas and put them in order, write your **first draft** as quickly as possible. Do not worry about wording, spelling, or other mechanics. Record your ideas on paper, on a computer disk, or even on magnetic tape. <u>Write on only one side of your paper</u>. If you later decide to reorganize your composition, you will be able to see the whole thing at once. You can even cut and paste if you want to. Obviously that is impossible if you have written on front and back. Skipping lines also simplifies revision. The important thing is to record your ideas.

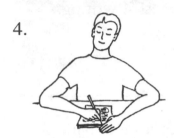

4. Once you have your ideas down, begin **polishing**. First consider *what* you are saying. Have you made your message clear and effective? Have you created vivid pictures that will bring your ideas to life? Is everything directed toward your purpose? Will your beginning get your readers' attention? Will your ending leave them with the thoughts and feelings you want them to have? Read your composition aloud, checking for smooth sentences.

5. Although you may have been **conferring** with others throughout the writing process, it is especially important to get feedback when you yourself are satisfied with your composition. Read your writing aloud, asking your listener to focus on the *content*, or message. Have your listener "tell back" what he or she heard. That lets you know how your piece comes across to someone else. Ask your listener what works well in your writing, and invite suggestions for improvement. That response will be much more helpful than just saying your writing is great as it is. If your listener is reluctant to give specific feedback, ask questions. If you are unsure of a particular section, call it to your listener's attention. Open-ended questions, rather than the yes-no variety, will give more information. For example, the answer to "What did this section mean to you?" is more helpful than the answer to "Was this part clear?" It might have been perfectly clear to your listener, but the message received might have been quite different from the message you intended.

6. Of course, it is *your* composition; you have the final say about which changes will be made and which things will remain as they are. However, you should at least **consider suggestions**. Your ideas are probably perfectly clear to you, but those people with whom you confer let you know how effectively your ideas come across *from your paper*. Their help is invaluable.

7. Once you are again satisfied with the content of your piece of writing, you are ready to begin **editing**, focusing on the mechanics. You might have done some of this in your earlier stages of polishing, but now you are editing in detail. Again it is helpful to focus on only one task at a time.

   a. First consider whether all of your **sentences** are complete.

   b. Then see whether you have started new **paragraphs** in the right places. You should start a new paragraph when you move on to a new topic or major segment of your composition. If you are writing conversation, you need to start a new paragraph whenever you change speakers.

   c. Third see if you have proper **usage** (subject–verb agreement, right form of verb, correct pronoun, etc.).

   d. Next check to see if your **capitalization** is correct. (If this is especially difficult for you, you might want to go through your composition once checking just for capitalization at the beginning of a sentence; then go through a second time checking for words that should be capitalized within sentences.)

   e. Fifth, check **punctuation**. You might want to subdivide this step also.

   f. Finally, check **spelling**. It's fine to use the feature on your word processing program that checks spelling, but don't let that be your only check. That will tell you only if your words are words; it will not tell you if they are the *right* words.

8. You are now ready to make what you hope will be your **final copy**. If you are handwriting your composition, you will need to repeat the proofreading steps described in Step 7. Using a word processor simplifies correction of errors. <u>Be sure to save your work frequently and to make one or more backup disks.</u>

9. **Share** your ideas—via your writing—with a broader audience. Enjoy your readers' responses.

PROOFREADER'S MARKS

Standardized proofreading symbols are understood by writers, editors, and typesetters. If you begin using these symbols now, you will be learning a small "language" that will enable you to communicate with many other people.

¶ This symbol marks the beginning of a **paragraph**. It should be placed exactly where the paragraph is to begin, not just in the margin.

≡ Three lines under one or more letters show that they are to be **capitalized**.

／ A slanted line going through a letter at this angle indicates that the letter is to be **lowercased**. If consecutive capitalized letters are to be lowercased, a horizontal line would extend from the top of this line above all letters to the right.

⋀ This symbol, called a **caret**, indicates where one or more letters or words should be **inserted**. (When a comma is inserted, a caret is usually placed above it so that it is more easily seen.) The inserted word or letter should be written *above* the line to which it is to be added. If there is not enough space above the line, find a place where there *is* space. If that is elsewhere on the page, neatly draw a line around the material to be inserted, and join it to the caret. If the material to be inserted must be written on a separate page, clearly label it *Insert 1*, *Insert A*, etc., and put a corresponding label at the point where the insertion is to be made.

⋁ This "upside-down caret" is used for **insertions** that would be **above the regular line of type**, such as apostrophes, quotation marks, and superior numerals for footnotes. The symbol to be added is written in the "v" of the caret.

℘ Commonly called the **delete** symbol, this mark indicates that one or more words, letters, or punctuation marks is to be **taken out**.

⌣ This symbol, which means to **close up space**, is often used with the delete symbol. After something has been deletcd, the space created needs to be closed. This symbol means to close space entirely. Using only the top part of the symbol means to close space partially, usually leaving space between remaining words.

This versatile symbol has several meanings. In editing it is used to show where **space** is to be inserted between words or between lines.

⊙ When a **period** is inserted, a circle is put around it so it is more easily seen.

As the curving of this symbol suggests, it indicates that letters or words are to be **transposed** (shifted so that their order is reversed).

This symbol would be placed at the point where a **new line** should start. You might use it when writing poetry, a quotation, a list, or something else that you want to set off.

Two parallel vertical lines indicate that two lines should be **aligned** or indented the same amount. This might be used to mark the heading of a letter.

Notice how these symbols are used to show editing changes in the following paragraph.

¶ Reading and experience can sometimes be blended in such a way that each is rich enriches the other er for their union. For example, Ray Bradbury's <u>Dandelion Wine</u> is most effectively read in summer. Hot, humid summer days help the reader to experience the atmosphere of an Illinois summer. Reading about Douglas's adventures experiences, which have aged in memory like bottles of dandelion wine in a wine cellar, helps us to become more aware of our own experiences in the days before air conditioning

Sometimes teachers put symbols in the lefthand margin of a paper to give students clues about the kinds of corrections that are needed. Unlike the proofreaders' symbols shown above, these symbols are not standard. They may vary from one teacher to another. Be sure to learn the system your teacher uses.

sp   Look for a **misspelled word**.

cap   Look for a **capitalization error**. This might be a word that is not capitalized and needs to be, or a word that is capitalized and shouldn't be.

p   Look for a **punctuation error**. This might be punctuation you need to add or punctuation you need to take away.

RO   Look for a **run-on sentence**. Although this is a type of punctuation error (and likely involves capitalization as well), it is such a common error that it often gets its own symbol.

frag   Look for a sentence **fragment**.

W   Look for a **wrong word**. It might be a wrong homophone (*to* for *too*, for example), a wrong verb form, or any of a number of other things.

?   Something is **unclear**. Look for writing that is illegible or ideas that don't seem to make sense.

The passage below has been marked as a teacher might mark it for student correction. Can you can figure out what needs to be changed? (A diagonal line is used to separate two corrections on one line.)

cap   One sure sign of Spring is the bird

sp   which each year tries to build it's

        nest in our mail slot. It announces

sp/P   it's arrival with shrill calls, and

frag

wildly flapping wings. When we
investigate. We find a collection
of twigs, dry grass, and an
assortment of other "building
materials." Once we even found a
plastic drinking straw! This is no

RO/sp dumb bird, it has probly picked the
best nesting spot for miles around.
What other bird has a brick nest

P   lined with metal.

FRIENDLY LETTERS

Writing letters can be a very rewarding experience. It gives you a
chance to share organized and polished ideas with another person or
perhaps, as in the case of a letter to a newspaper editor, with the rest
of the community. For many people, the most rewarding part of
letter-writing is getting a response—whether that be a personal letter
in their mailbox or a change in public policy.

The example on the next page shows the parts of a friendly letter.
The **heading** lets your reader know when the letter was written and
where a reply should be sent. If someone knows you very well, however, or if you correspond regularly, you may omit your address.

The **closing**, also called the complimentary close, shows your relationship to the reader or the attitude with which you send the letter.
There are many appropriate closings, such as *Sincerely, Yours truly,
Fondly, Your friend, Your pen pal,* or *Your cousin.* Notice that
neither *From* nor *Thank you* is an appropriate closing. If you want
to thank your reader, you should do so in the body of your letter.
Notice also that the closing is followed by a comma and that only the
first letter of the first word is capitalized.

The following thank-you note illustrates the form of a friendly
letter. It is followed by an appropriately addressed envelope.

8721 Sierra Drive
(HEADING) St. Louis, MO 63117
November 3, 1997

(SALUTATION or
Dear Grandma and Grandpa, *GREETING)*

B   Thanks for the beautiful pink sweater you sent
me for my birthday. It's my favorite color and looks
O great with the navy slacks and print blouse I got from
Mom.
D   I can't wait to see you on Thanksgiving. It's such
fun to sit around the table and hear about the things
Y Mom did with Aunt Ellie and Uncle Frank when
they were kids. I'll see you soon!

(CLOSING) Love,

(SIGNATURE) Crystal

Crystal Meyer
8721 Sierra Drive
St. Louis, MO 63117

Mr. and Mrs. Stephen Graham

2937 Pembroke Way

Memphis, TN 38129

BUSINESS LETTERS

The main difference between a business letter and a friendly letter is that a business letter relates to business (or school) matters rather than to personal matters. For that reason, and because a business letter often is written to someone with whom the writer is not acquainted, it is <u>more formal</u> than a friendly letter. Here are some guidelines for writing effective business letters.

1. Make every effort to send your letter to a **specific person** rather than use the general salutation *Dear Sir* or *To whom it may concern*. This often increases your chances of getting a favorable reply. If you do not know the name of the person to whom you should write, you can usually find out by telephoning the company. While you're on the phone, check the spelling of the person's name; even common names can have unusual spellings.

2. Be sure that your letter has only **one purpose**. Everything in your letter should be geared toward getting a particular response. If you have two purposes, you will cut your effectiveness in half.

| refund | order | job | sale | info |

3. Keep your letter **short**. Short paragraphs will make it easier for your busy reader to identify your main points. Some paragraphs in your letter might have only one sentence.

4. Make yourself **clear**. Directly (and politely) state exactly what you would like the reader to do. You're more likely to get what you want if the reader doesn't have to read your mind.

5. Most business transactions benefit both parties: When a customer makes a purchase, a business makes a sale; when a person applies for a job, a company may get a valuable employee. However, if

your letter requests a favor and the person or business will in no way benefit, you should enclose a self-addressed stamped envelope (**SASE**). It greatly increases the possibility of your receiving a prompt reply. SASEs are often appropriate for letters requesting information. The writer of our example business letter did not enclose one because he was writing to a Chamber of Commerce. His project on Portland would help the Chamber of Commerce achieve its goal of publicizing the city.

6. Write the letter neatly in **standard form**.

In addition to the parts of a friendly letter, a business letter contains an **inside address**. That is the name and address of *the person to whom you are writing*. It is identical to the main address on the envelope. The inside address helps the letter get to the right person, even when the letter is separated from the envelope.

Dear in the salutation may seem overly affectionate for a business letter. However, it is merely a formality. Use the person's name as you would if you were speaking to him or her. Usually you would use a title and a last name, such as *Ms. MacLean* or *Dr. Chin*. If the first name is such that you cannot tell whether the person is a man or a woman, it is fine to use both names—for example, *Dear Leslie Russell*. Notice that the salutation is followed by a colon rather than a comma as in the friendly letter. This is part of the letter's formality.

Sincerely or *Yours truly* is a good closing for a business letter. As in the friendly letter, the closing is followed by a comma, and only the first letter of the first word is capitalized. If your business letter is typed, your name should be typed four spaces below the closing. That ensures that the reader will be able to read your name. You should sign your name (in cursive) in the space below the closing.

The preceding points about a business letter are illustrated in the example on the next page.

9847 Sheridan Lake Road
(HEADING)   Rapid City, SD 57718
September 22, 1997

Ms. Diane Larsen, Director
Portland Chamber of Commerce *(INSIDE*
221 NW 2nd Avenue *ADDRESS)*
Portland, OR 97209

Dear Ms. Larsen: *(SALUTATION* or *GREETING)*

B The theme for my school's social studies fair this
year is "River Cities." I have chosen to do my project
on Portland.

O Please send me information related to this topic. I am
especially interested in how the river contributed to
Portland's population growth and how the river is
important to the city's major industries. Are the
D industries that were responsible for Portland's early
growth still important today?

I would appreciate receiving this information as soon
Y as possible since I am eager to get an early start on
my project. Thank you very much for your help.

(CLOSING)   Yours truly,

(SIGNATURE)   *Brian Jensen*

Brian Jensen

FOLDING THE LETTER

Once you have written your letter, you need to neatly get it into its addressed envelope. The edges of the paper should align after the paper is folded, and the thickness of the letter should be uniform; one side should not be bulkier than the other.

Believe it or not, a letter on 8 1/2- by 11-inch paper can fit neatly into an envelope that is either 4 1/8 inches by 9 1/2 inches, or 3 5/8 inches by 6 1/2 inches (or variations thereof). Folding for the longer envelope is one step shorter. (Some letters that come to your home may be folded differently from this because they may have been folded for a window envelope or folded by machine. This is still the method you should use.) Basically, you are making two folds to fold your letter approximately into thirds.

1. Lay the envelope with the address side down and the flap up.

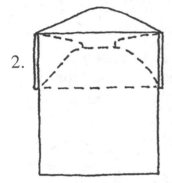

2. Put the top of your letter face up under the flap so that the top of the paper is against the fold. Be sure the paper is against the fold *all the way across*.

3. Move the bottom of the letter up beyond the top of the envelope so that you can see about 1/4 inch of the envelope below the letter. <u>Be sure the sides of the letter align</u>. Crease.

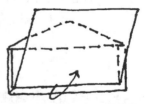

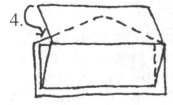

4. Move the bottom of the letter toward the inside of the crease you just made. About 1/4 inch should be showing at the top of the letter. Again align the sides of your letter. Crease.

5. Slide the letter into the envelope so that the top of the letter is at the top of the envelope and the top front of the letter is toward the back of the envelope. This will be very convenient for the person who opens the letter.

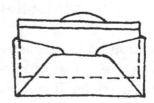

Letters on 8 1/2- by 11-inch paper often look very messy when they come out of 3 5/8- by 6 1/2-inch envelopes. They needn't. You will be making three folds for this letter. The first two steps are identical to folding for the long envelope.

1. Lay the envelope with the address side down and the flap up.

2. Put the top of your letter face up under the flap so that the top of the paper is against the fold. Be sure the paper is against the fold *all the way across*.

3. 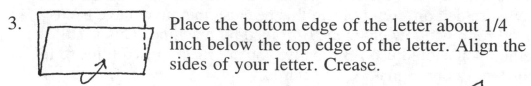 Place the bottom edge of the letter about 1/4 inch below the top edge of the letter. Align the sides of your letter. Crease.

4. With the letter folded nearly in half, move the left side of the letter so that it is about 3 inches from the right edge of the letter. Align the edges. Crease.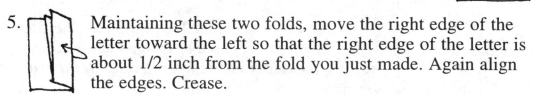

5. 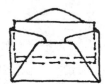 Maintaining these two folds, move the right edge of the letter toward the left so that the right edge of the letter is about 1/2 inch from the fold you just made. Again align the edges. Crease.

6. Slip the letter into the envelope so that the top front of the letter is toward the back of the envelope and the top of the letter is toward the left.

MAKING A BIBLIOGRAPHY

A bibliography is a list of references used in preparing a project or report. Two main purposes of a bibliography are to give credit to your sources and to tell readers where they can double-check your information or find out more about your topic. Be sure that information in your bibliography is <u>accurate</u> and as <u>complete</u> as possible.

As soon as you realize that a source contains information that you might use in your report, you should take down that source's bibliographic data. It will be much more efficient to get the information immediately than to risk having to try to find the source again, perhaps after you have returned it to a library.

The information given about each source makes up a bibliography **entry**. Entries should be arranged in <u>alphabetical order</u> according to their first letter. They should *not be numbered*. <u>Runover lines</u> within an entry should be <u>indented</u>. The entire bibliography should be <u>double-spaced</u>. The preferred title for this page, which usually appears at the end of your report, is Works Cited (rather than Bibliography). That title emphasizes that these are sources you really used, not just sources that would have information on your topic.

There are several correct ways to arrange information within a bibliography entry. You should consistently follow one of the acceptable styles. Style recommendations for online entries are frequently changing.

The following examples show the most commonly used bibliography entries. The style used for all entries except those of the online sources is the one recommended by the Modern Language Association (MLA). This style is used for most general writing. Other styles may be recommended for research in specialized fields. After studying these examples, you would probably be able to make a good guess at an appropriate style for a different type of entry. You could also consult a reference book that gives more detailed information about writing research papers.

The parts of each entry are first listed with appropriate punctuation between them. Then an example of that type of entry is given. Although punctuation marks are emphasized here, you should use regular text type for your punctuation. MLA style calls for underlining titles even though italic type may be available.

Book With One Author

Author (last name first). <u>Title</u>. City: Publisher, Copyright.

Lederer, Richard. <u>The Miracle of Language</u>. New York: Pocket
    Books, 1991.

The publisher is usually found near the bottom of the title page. If more than one city is listed there, choose the one closest to you. The publication date is usually found on the back of the title page. Sometimes more than one date is listed. Use the original date unless the work has been revised. Then use the original date after the title and the date of the revision you are using at the end of the entry.

Book With Two Authors

Newman, Mildred, and Bernard Berkowitz. How To Be Your Own Best Friend. New York: Random House, 1971.

Notice that the first name of the second author is given before the last name.

Encyclopedia Entry

"Entry," Title of Encyclopedia, edition.

"Acupuncture," The World Book Encyclopedia, 1997 ed.

Magazine Article

Author (last name first). "Article Title." Magazine Title. Date (day Month year): pages.

Westrup, Hugh. "Riddle of the Flying Reptiles." Current Science. 21 March 1997: 4-7.

If no author is given, start with the title of the article. Alphabetize all entries by first letter.

Personal Interview

Name. Personal interview. Date (day Month year).

Chang, Cheryl. Personal interview. 6 June 1998.

Television Program

"Title of Episode." <u>Title of Program</u>. Title of Series (if applicable). Name of network. Call letters, City of local station. Broadcast date (day Month year).

"Treasures of the Sunken City." <u>Nova</u>. PBS. KETC, St. Louis. 18 November 1997.

Portable Database (CD-ROM, Diskette, Magnetic Tape, etc.)

Author (if available). "Title of article, entry, story, poem, etc." <u>Title of Product</u>. Edition, release, or version. Medium. City of Publication: Publisher, Date.

Garst, Ronald D. "Kenya." <u>Grolier Multimedia Encyclopedia</u>. Version 7.0.2. CD-ROM. Grolier Electronic Publishing, Inc., 1995.

Notice that when a piece of information in the bibliography entry is not available (a city in the entry above), it is simply skipped.

Online Sources: E-mail

Author. <Author's e-mail address>. "Subject line of message." Personal e-mail. Date (day Month year).

Green, Cindy. <cgreen56@aol.com>. "Family History." Personal e-mail. 14 April 1998.

When including e-mail addresses or URL (Uniform Resource Locator) addresses, be sure they are accurate. Double-check all letters, punctuation marks, capitalization, etc. Enclosing an online address in < > will help to separate it from the rest of the entry. If the address is to be followed with punctuation, be sure that the punctuation is *outside* the closing > so that it does not look like part of the address.

Online Sources: Web Site

Author. "Title of Document." <u>Publication</u>. Date of publication or last revision. <URL>. Date of access (day Month year).

Lynds, Beverly T. <u>About Rainbows</u>. 19 September 1995. <http://www.unidata.ucar.edu/staff/blynds/rnbw.html>. 5 January 1998.

If your information is from an electronic version of material (such as a magazine) that also appears in print, the first part of your entry should be a bibliography entry for the print version. Immediately follow that, on the same line, with the information specified above. If any part of the information does not pertain to your source or is unavailable, just go on to the next piece of information that you have. <u>*Date of access* for online sources is especially important since the materials, unlike books, may be changed frequently</u>.

FOOTNOTES

There are two kinds of footnotes. **Content footnotes** give helpful information that might be too interruptive if included in the body of your report. Definitions are examples of content footnotes. Content footnotes should be used sparingly because they can distract and annoy the reader. Before you write a footnote, ask yourself whether the information is important. If you decide that it is, consider whether you could include it in the body of your report rather than in a footnote. You can find examples of content footnotes in this book at the bottom of the irregular verb charts on pages 39-41.

The second kind of footnote is a **reference footnote**. While a bibliography lists a researcher's sources, reference footnotes tell which information came from which source. <u>Any source you cite in a footnote should also be included in your bibliography</u>.

Inexperienced researchers often wonder which material they need to footnote. If you use someone else's exact words, you need to put those words in quotation marks and indicate your source. (You should always put ideas into your own words unless the original author's exact wording is necessary.) There are many times, however, when you should give credit for an *idea* even though you have used your own *words*. <u>Generally, unless information is a commonly known fact, a commonly shared opinion, or your original idea, you should indicate your source</u>. Citing an authority supports your point.

Footnotes are much simpler to use than they used to be. They used to be placed at the bottom of the page containing the information to which they referred (hence, the name *foot*notes). This often created a nightmare for typists. Today footnotes, often called *end*notes, may appear at the end of the entire paper instead of at the bottom of each page. They should start on a <u>new page</u>, titled *Notes*, and should be <u>numbered consecutively</u> throughout your report. On the Notes page, the number of the note should be <u>slightly above the line</u> (as it is in the report itself). It should be followed by a <u>space but no punctuation</u>. Endnotes should be <u>double-spaced</u>.

Footnotes used to include the same information as bibliography entries. However, it was arranged a little differently, causing confusion for the writer. Here is an example of the long form for a footnote.

[1] Richard Lederer, <u>The Miracle of Language</u>

(New York: Pocket Books, 1991) 19.

The number at the end is a page number (page numbers of books do not appear in a bibliography). If you study this example and compare it with the bibliography entry for the same source on page 131, you will probably be able to figure out how to convert your bibliography entries to footnotes.

Today, rather than appearing at the bottom of the page or at the end of the report, "footnotes" are often included in parentheses within the body of the report. This is easier for both the writer and the reader. The notes identify the source of the information while interrupting the text as little as possible. <u>Include a page number</u> and only enough information to identify the source in your bibliography. Notice various short forms for the note cited earlier.

(Lederer 19) (This most common form would follow Mr. Lederer's idea in the body of the report.)

(19) (Only the page number would be used if Mr. Lederer's name had been included in the body of the report in relation to the cited material.)

(R. Lederer 19) (If your bibliography includes works by two or more authors named *Lederer*, you would use the initial to identify the one you meant.)

(Lederer, *Miracle* 19) (If your bibliography includes two works by Lederer, you would use a shortened form of the title to indicate the source you are citing.)

Even more important than using proper *form* for footnotes is giving credit where it is due. Passing off someone else's ideas as your own is called **plagiarism**. It is against the law. Students are sometimes expelled from schools for plagiarism.

WRITING STYLE: ACTIVE AND PASSIVE VOICE

As you write more (and read more), you will probably want to become an even better writer. One way to make your writing livelier and more direct is to use **active voice**. In active voice the subject of the sentence performs an action.

Amy scored a goal.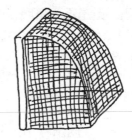

In **passive voice** the subject is acted upon by some other agent.

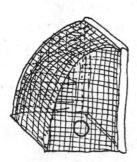

A goal was scored by Amy.

A goal was scored.

If the person or thing performing the action is indicated at all, it will be in a prepositional phrase beginning with *by*. The doer of the action has less importance than in active voice when it is the subject of the sentence. In passive voice the verb will always be *at least* two words (a form of "to be" plus a past participle). Passive voice, therefore, requires more words than does active voice.

<u>Passive voice may occur in past, present, or future tense.</u>

> *Dinner **was cooked** by Dad.* (passive voice, past tense)

> *Dad **cooked** dinner.* (active voice, past tense)

> *Most of our milk **is produced** by cows.* (passive voice, present tense)

> *Cows **produce** most of our milk.* (active voice, present tense)

> *Refreshments **will be brought** by the sixth graders.* (passive voice, future tense)

> *The sixth graders **will bring** refreshments.* (active voice, future tense)

<u>Usually it is better to use active voice in your writing</u>. It is shorter, livelier, and more direct. There are a few times, however, when passive voice is better.

> *The bank **was robbed**.* (The doer of the action is unknown.)

> *The temperature **was varied**.* (The action itself is much more important than the person or thing performing it. A report of a science experiment is one situation in which passive voice is preferable.)

WRITING STYLE: SENTENCE VARIETY

Your writing will be more interesting and more effective if you vary the length and pattern of your sentences. In your reading, when you come across a sentence with an interesting structure, jot it down, also noting where you found it. You might want to begin a notebook for sentence structures, words, and other ideas that you would like to use in your writing.

In addition to the discussion of sentences on pages 16 to 30, the following examples show some of the many ways to vary your sentences. Numbers in parentheses indicate pages in this book where additional information can be found.

1. Write an interrogative sentence (a question). (page 24)

   Why can't the world's problems hit us at eighteen, when we know everything? (Anonymous)

2. Write an imperative sentence (a command). (page 24)

   Learn as much by writing as by reading. (Lord Acton, English historian, 1834–1902)

3. Write an exclamatory sentence. (page 24)

   How many good books suffer neglect through the inefficiency of their beginnings! (Edgar Allan Poe, U.S. writer, 1809–1849)

4. Write a direct quotation. (pages 80–81)

   "Give me liberty, or give me death!" proclaimed Patrick Henry. (American patriot, orator, and statesman, 1736–1799)

5. Write a compound sentence. (pages 18–19)

   I disapprove of what you say, but I will defend to the death your right to say it. (Voltaire, French philosopher and writer, 1694–1778)

6. Write a complex sentence. (pages 19–20)

The finest thought runs the risk of being irretrievably forgotten if it is not written down. (Arthur Schopenhauer, German philosopher, 1788–1860)

7. Write a compound–complex sentence. (pages 20–21)

You may be disappointed if you fail, but you are doomed if you don't try. (Beverly Sills, U.S. opera singer, born 1929)

8. Write a sentence with an appositive. (pages 74–75)

*Every great mistake has a halfway moment, **a split-second when it can be recalled and perhaps remedied.*** (Pearl S. Buck, U.S. writer, 1892–1973)

9. Write a sentence with a restrictive clause. (page 77)

*People **who fly into a rage** always make a bad landing.* (Will Rogers, U.S. humorist, 1879–1935)

10. Write a sentence with a non-restrictive clause. (pages 76–77)

*Turkey vultures, **which cruise hundreds of feet above the dense rain forests of South America**, use their sense of smell to find food on the forest floor.*

11. Begin a sentence with a prepositional phrase. (pages 10–12)

***For children**, leaf fall is just one of the odder figments of Nature, like hailstones or snowflakes.* (*A Natural History of the Senses* by Diane Ackerman, U.S. writer, b. 1948)

12. Begin a sentence with an adverb. (pages 9–10)

Sideways, spinning, the sled hit a bump in the hill and Jonas was jarred loose and thrown violently into the air. (*The Giver* by Lois Lowry, U.S. writer, b. 1937)

13. Begin a sentence with an adjective that is separated from the noun it modifies by a verb.

*How **thin** and **sharp** and ghostly **white**
Is the slim curved crook of the moon tonight.*
(Langston Hughes, U.S. writer, 1902–1967)

14. Begin a sentence with a direct object. (page 28)

***Courage** had she for the task that was before her.*

15. Use a present infinitive as a subject. (page 37)

***To lose patience** is to lose the battle.* (Mohandas K. Gandhi, Indian spiritual and political leader, 1869–1948)

16. Use a perfect infinitive as a subject.

***To have become a deeper man** is the privilege of those who have suffered.* (Oscar Wilde, Irish writer, 1854–1900)

17. Begin a sentence with a participle (an *-ing* word used as an adjective).

***Grunting, hissing**, a dozen buses pulled up behind me and threw open their doors.* (*High Tide in Tucson* by Barbara Kingsolver, U.S. writer, b. 1955)

18. Use a gerund (an -*ing* word used as a noun).

   ***Stumbling** is the fruit of haste.* (Jane Austen, English writer, 1775–1817).

19. Use a noun clause, in this case used as a direct object.

   ***Whose woods these are**, I think I know.* (Robert Frost, U.S. poet, 1874–1963)

20. Write a periodic sentence, which builds suspense by delaying the independent clause to the end of the sentence, preceding it with other clauses and phrases.

   As far as the eye could see, all around, wherever I looked, snow was lifting and spiraling from the steppe. (The Endless Steppe by Esther Hautzig, Polish-born U.S. writer, b. 1930)

21. Write a simile, a comparison that uses the word *like* or *as*.

   Hating people is like burning down your own house to get rid of a rat. (Harry Emerson Fosdick, U.S. preacher and author, 1878–1969)

22. Write a metaphor, a comparison that says one thing *is* another.

   Service is the rent that you pay for room on this earth. (Shirley Chisolm, U.S. politician, b. 1924)

APPENDIX:
TIPS FOR SUCCESS IN SCHOOL

HOMEWORK

The following suggestions will help you to be successful with your homework.

1. 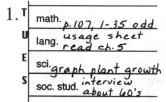 Write down each **assignment**. It is helpful to have an assignment notebook for this purpose and to write each assignment *on the day it is due*. That will help you as you plan your time and decide what you should work on first.

2. Be sure to take home all the **materials**—textbooks, notebooks, tools, etc.—that you will need to complete your assignments.

3. Have a particular **place** where you regularly do your homework. This place should be well lit and should be equipped with any supplies you might need, such as a dictionary, thesaurus, pencil sharpener, etc. Your study area should also be free of distractions, especially television.

4.  As much as possible, do your homework at the same **time** each day. Find out what works best for you. Do you work most efficiently if you do your homework right after school, or do you work better if you have a break first? Do you work better if you have a large block of time, or do you need frequent breaks, even of a few minutes? Is it better for you to do your hardest subject first when you are fresh or to save it for last when you can give it your full attention? People will have different answers to these questions.

5. **Review** your notes each evening. If anything is unclear, check it yourself or ask your teacher or one of your classmates about it. This will make test preparation much easier for you.

6. **Practice** oral presentations in front of a mirror and then in front of a live audience. A few people are best, but a pet is better than no one.

CLASS PARTICIPATION

Participating wholeheartedly in class will help you to learn more efficiently. Then you will probably have to spend less time doing homework.

1. Arrive at class prepared. That means that your homework is finished, you have all materials you need, and you are mentally

prepared for the class activity. You will feel confident and will be able to add to your knowledge of the subject.

2. Notice what the focus of the lesson is, and work toward the class's group goal. If the class is talking about the Louisiana Purchase, for example, don't bring up for discussion a souvenir that you bought during Mardi Gras in New Orleans.

3. Think about how today's lesson relates to other lessons you have had in this class recently—or to lessons you *will* have, if you know what they are.

4. Be involved in class. Give the activity or the discussion your full attention. Remember, however, that your involvement should not interfere with the involvement of your classmates. Participation in discussion, for example, involves *listening* as well as speaking.

5. If oral participation is difficult for you, set a goal of participating once or twice each class. Then force yourself to do it. It's fine to answer questions even if you're not sure of the answer. You may find that you're right more often than you expect to be, and even if you're wrong, you'll probably learn something. At any rate, participation will get easier as you do more of it.

6. Be sure to ask a classmate or your teacher about anything that is unclear, either content being studied or requirements of an assignment. If you ask a classmate, choose someone who is informed.

TEST PREPARATION

1. Be totally involved in each class, and complete all assignments promptly and carefully.

2. Be sure to keep all notes and handouts in order. A looseleaf binder with dividers labeled for each subject generally works well.

3. Look over your notes each evening (even before a test is announced). Get clarification of anything you don't understand.

4. If there are things you need to memorize, such as capitals, dates, vocabulary, etc., begin as soon as the assignment is made. Divide the task into parts, memorizing some items each day.

5. Pay careful attention to any information your teacher gives you about the test. Be sure you know what material is to be covered and what type of question will be asked. Each type of question—matching, true-false, completion, or essay—requires slightly different preparation.

6. Begin studying for the test as soon as it is announced. Don't wait until the night before.

7. Complete any review sheets the teacher gives you. Do as much as possible without your textbook or notes; then be sure to check your answers carefully.

8. Write down some questions that you think will be asked on the test. You might exchange questions with a classmate for some test-taking practice.

9. If the test will have one or more essay questions, practice writing an essay answer. The teacher might tell you ahead of time exactly what an essay question will be so that you can prepare a good response. Even if the teacher doesn't tell you, you might be able to guess what the teacher will ask you to write about. What did the teacher seem to consider important as you studied the chapter? Jot down some notes so that you can present complete information in an organized way. Be sure to put material into your own words. Check your essay for factual accuracy. Proofread it according to the guidelines on page 119. If you needed to refer to your textbook or notes often while writing your essay, repeat this exercise until you can write independently.

10. Sometimes it works well to have a parent, sibling, or classmate quiz you over the material to be covered on the test. If this is not convenient—or if you want to study more independently— prepare note cards or a two-column study sheet so that you can quiz yourself. If you are studying definitions, for example, write the word on one side of a note card and the definition on the other side. Or write the word in a lefthand column and the

definition to the right. You will then be able to cover half the material, quiz yourself, and check to see if you are right. Many types of factual material can be studied in this way.

11. Get a good night's sleep, and eat a good breakfast.

TEST TAKING

If you have been involved in class and have been doing your homework, a test is an opportunity to show what you have learned and to find out what you still need to study.

1. Take time to read the directions. No matter how well you know the material, if you do the wrong thing, you might get a very low score.

2. Budget your time. If you are stuck on one item, don't waste too much time on it. Instead go on to other items, and go back to the difficult one later.

3. Read test questions carefully. The word *not*, for example, totally changes the meaning of a sentence.

4. See if the test itself can help you with troublesome items. For example, if you have to list fifteen prepositions and you can think of only twelve, maybe you can find some on the test.

5. When you have completed your test, take time to recheck your answers. Don't just *reread* the test, *rethink* it.

6. When you get your graded test back, be sure to gain an understanding of items you missed. Consider whether you should do anything differently in preparing for or taking the next test.

INDEX

Numbers in parentheses indicate a numbered item on the page listed.

148

ORDER FORM

Please send me _____ copies of *Hands-On English*
@ $9.95 _____

Other items (Visit <www.porticobooks.com> to see if new items are available.) _____

If you are ordering 6 or more items, give yourself a 15% discount. _____

MO residents, add 7.225% sales tax* _____

Shipping/Delivery charges ($3.00 for the first book; $0.50 for each additional book) _____

TOTAL _____

☐ Check or money order enclosed.
☐ Bill my credit card.   ☐ Master Card   ☐ Visa

_____   _____ / _____
Credit Card Number   mo.   yr.
                     Expiration date

Print name on credit card _____

Print cardholder's address _____

_____

Authorized signature _____

Mail orders: **P. O. Box 9451, St. Louis, MO 63117**
Fax orders: **(314) 721-7131**   **Phone** orders **(314) 721-7131**
            (toll free) 1 (888) 641-5353
     You are welcome to photocopy this form.

*If you have a tax-exempt status, please enclose a copy of your tax letter.

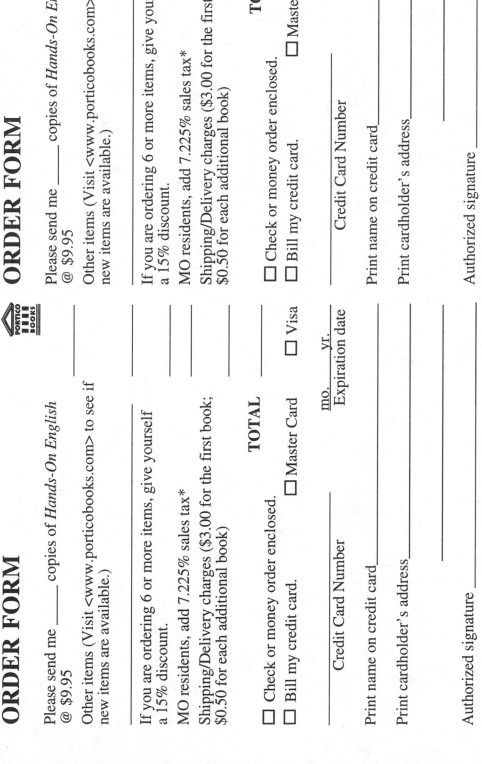

ORDER FORM

Please send me _____ copies of *Hands-On English*
@ $9.95 _____

Other items (Visit <www.porticobooks.com> to see if new items are available.) _____

If you are ordering 6 or more items, give yourself a 15% discount. _____

MO residents, add 7.225% sales tax* _____

Shipping/Delivery charges ($3.00 for the first book; $0.50 for each additional book) _____

TOTAL _____

☐ Check or money order enclosed.
☐ Bill my credit card.   ☐ Master Card   ☐ Visa

_____   _____ / _____
Credit Card Number   mo.   yr.
                     Expiration date

Print name on credit card _____

Print cardholder's address _____

_____

Authorized signature _____

Mail orders: **P. O. Box 9451, St. Louis, MO 63117**
Fax orders: **(314) 721-7131**   **Phone** orders **(314) 721-7131**
            (toll free) 1 (888) 641-5353
     You are welcome to photocopy this form.

*If you have a tax-exempt status, please enclose a copy of your tax letter.